SUICIDE

THE IRISH EXPERIENCE

Seán Spellissy

ON STREAM

Published 1996 by On Stream Publications Ltd. Cloghroe, Blarney, Co. Cork, Ireland.Tel/Fax 021 385798

ISBN: 1 897685 87 4

Printed in Ireland by Colour Books.

The Author

Seán Spellissy is an historian whose previous publications include:

Clare County of Contrast (1987)

Limerick The Rich Land (1989)

A Portrait of Ennis (1990)

He has edited a number of publications including:

The Other Clare, Vol. 9, 1985

The Other Clare, Vol. 10 (1986)

The Royal O'Briens, 1992.

He is the member of an old Ennis family and runs The Book Gallery, a secondhand bookshop in Ennis, Co.Clare.

DEDICATED TO FRIEND WHO CHOSE DEATH

Ar scáth a chéile is eadh mhairid na daoine.

Seán-fhocal

People live in one another's shadow.

Proverb.

CONTENTS

FOREWORD

Suicide is now viewed as an 'acceptable' means of death by the community and is the second commonest cause of death in the fifteen to thirty- four year old age group. The causation is variable and cannot all be attributable to depression which is the primary cause of suicide in an elderly population. It occurs suddenly and unexpectedly and affects all members of the family, friends and community. It stigmatises the family, affects generations to come and with every suicide at least forty persons are immediately affected.

Because of the suddenness of suicide the grieving process takes longer, at least two to three years, and is harder to accept. The family has a sense of failure that permits others to commit suicide in the future.

This is not a clinical book nor does it look at suicide from a medical perspective. It contains views that are expressed verbally on a daily basis but rarely written about, and will encourage the reader to remember the facts or to seek further details in whatever aspect is stimulated.

Dr. Moosajee Bhamjee.

A Sudden Violent Death or a Tragical Fate

- A NICER WAY OF SAYING SUICIDE.

The fireside tales told by countless storytellers over the centuries may have influenced the way in which Irish people thought of various subjects, particularly suicide. Country people seem to have accepted self-killing in a very matter-of-fact manner. Victims of suicide were simply buried, quietly and without any fuss, in unconsecrated ground, and few people referred to what had happened. This quiet acceptance or resignation may be attributed to our Celtic heritage which seems to have been quite fatalistic about *anbhás* or *an-íd*.

Anbhás means a sudden violent death and is a derivative of *anbha*, prodigious, great or terrible, and *bás,* death. *Thug sé anbhás air féin,* he took a sudden violent death upon himself, means he committed suicide. This is the term for self-killing supplied by Rev. Patrick S. Dinneen (1860-1934) in his definitive Irish-English dictionary.

An-íd. an-íde or *anaoid*, mean a tragical fate, mutilation, ill-treatment or death, according to his definition. He believed that all three were derivatives of the word *oidheadh*, an act of slaying, death by violence, doom, fate, destiny, tragedy or what one deserves. *Thug sé an-íd air féin*, he took a tragical fate on himself, can also mean he committed suicide.

Suicide derives its English name from the Latin *sui,* of himself, and *cidium*, a variant of *caedere*, to kill.

The English word *suicide* makes its first appearance in Sir Thomas Browne's *Religio Medici* which was written in 1635 and published in 1642. It was not mentioned in Dr. Johnson's dictionary of 1755 but seems to have passed into general usage from the late eighteenth century onward. In 1850 John Ogilvie published his *Imperial Dictionary* which defined suicide as self-murder, the act of designedly destroying one's own life. All of Ireland was then part of the British Empire and subject to the same laws as England.

Under Irish law suicide was regarded as a felonious homicide, on a par with murder, manslaughter and infanticide. Attempted suicide was a felony, and suicide was deemed self-murder, or *felonia de se*. The Criminal Law (Suicide) Act became law in 1993 and this decriminalised suicide or attempted suicide, making Ireland the last country in Europe to do so. Suicide has not been considered a crime in England since 1961 but it is still a punishable offense to aid, abet, counsel or procure the suicide or attempted suicide of another in either Ireland or England.

Felo de se means 'he who kills' and was an unusual term under the old laws as it defined the criminal rather than the crime. The description of self-killing in the dictionary summarises the law and attitudes of that period:

Suicide, in a legal sense, can only be committed by a person of years of discretion and of sound mind. It is by the law of England, a crime, the legal effect of which is forfeiture to the crown of all the personal property which the party had at the time of death including debts due to him, but it is not attended with forfeiture of freehold or corruption of blood. In order to vest these in the crown, the fact of self-murder must be proved by an inquisition.

In Scots law, suicide draws after it the falling of the single escheat, or forfeiture to the crown of the person's movable estate. Proof of the self-murder may be sought in an action before the Court of Session, at the instance of the queen's donatory, against the executors of the deceased.

Parasuicide is the term for a non-fatal act of deliberate self-injury which is best interpreted as a desperate cry for help. This is usually done on impulse, often with the intention of dying. It can be motivated by anger, stress, frustration, loss of self-esteem or tension and is a common reaction amongst young people, particularly girls between the ages of fifteen and nineteen.

Attempted suicide has never been a punishable offence in Scotland.

Even so, the bodies of criminals, suicides and dead foundlings were routinely delivered up for dissection in Edinburgh from the sixteenth century onwards. By 1711, however, there were not enough bodies available to the medical schools so body-snatching became a profitable business.

In Ireland a bill that allowed for the post-execution dissection of all criminals came into effect in 1791. Susannah Killeen of Belfast was the first executed woman whose body was dissected in September of that year and Michael Moloney of Ennis was probably the last man so treated on 7 March 1832. *The Anatomy Act of 1832* ensured an adequate supply of bodies for the various medical institutions. I was, however, unable to find any record of the bodies of suicides being given up for dissection. In all probability those whose bodies were not identified and claimed may have been dissected, whether they were suicides or not.

In 1907 Mrs. Wyse Power, one of the North Dublin Guardians, noted that an excessive amount of unclaimed bodies, forty in all, had been sent to medical schools, over a three month period, by the master of the workhouse. He and the doctor had received twenty-five pence each for every unclaimed body and the porter who delivered them got twelve-and-a-half pence per corpse.

The Dublin Journal of Medical and Chemical Science carried an article on suicide in March 1836. This was written by J. Morrison and dealt with two cases. In one instance nitric acid had been poured into the ear with fatal consequences. The second case dealt with an attempted suicide in which the victim's epiglottis, the erect cartilage at the root of the tongue, had been divided.

The Anatomy of Suicide by F. Winslow was reviewed in the *Dublin University Magazine* in September 1841 and the motives and mysteries of suicide were the subject of another article in the *Irish Quarterly Review* of March, 1857. It and other problems were mentioned in the university magazine of April, 1880 and William Allan wrote of a case of suicide, which involved butting the head against a stone wall in the issue of the *Dublin Journal of Medical Science* for March 1886.

11

In 1994 Fergal Bowers published *Suicide in Ireland* and wrote of 3,134 deaths that had been officially classed as suicide between 1982 and 1992. He reported on the research conducted by Dr. Niamh Nic Daeid which showed that men were three times more likely to kill themselves than women and commented on how the number of people taking their own lives, in Ireland, has risen from seven per hundred thousand to ten per hundred thousand, a figure based on official statistics. The actual number of people who die by their own hands may be significantly higher as social workers, psychiatrists and others believe that official statistics are only the tip of the iceberg.

Suicide has been described by Erwin Stengel as the most personal action an individual can make, defining it as an act of aggression against others, even though self-directed. He mentioned it was a specifically human problem, that animals may die because of their behaviour but lack man's self- destructive urge. Stengel maintains that there is no period of history in which suicides did not occur, and found the English word *suicide* to be objectionable as it described both the victim and the act.

He recorded how man's ability to take life, his own or another's, was a human freedom, giving man an illusion of being in control of his own destiny, and offering mankind a certain comfort insofar as people could kill themselves if life became intolerable. He qualified the latter statement by adding that man had only a limited control over his urges, including his tendency for self-preservation, and nobody knows how he or she will react to physical or mental stress.

In the 1960s medical men received some of their information on mental health and suicide from publications such as *A Short Guide to Mental Illness for the Family Doctor* (1966). Its writer noted how many "unstable individuals" attempted suicide when under stress and mentioned how others attempted suicide or threatened to use it as a weapon in interpersonal conflict:

> It has been suggested that the unsuccessful suicide is in fact successful because his behaviour leads to friends and relatives coming to his aid. Such an attempt can be regarded as a cry for help.

However, it is difficult to be sure that most unsuccessful efforts set out with this purpose.

Even those who attempt suicide in order to bring attention to themselves and to their plight may in fact be desperately unhappy and desire death. It is difficult in many cases to estimate the seriousness of intent. It is often argued that the person who does not take adequate steps to prevent discovery is not really intending to commit suicide. However, this may be because the agitated depressive, even though determined to kill himself, is unable to think out his plan in sufficient detail because of his intense anxiety.

It is difficult to assess the risk of suicide in this kind of depression. It is essential to ask every depressed patient if he has thoughts of suicide and if he has considered any particular means to this end. Most textbooks state that endogenous depressives (those whose depression appears to come from within) with marked self reproach are the most likely to attempt suicide, because they believe they are unfit to live. The only factor which correlates meaningfully with suicide and attempted suicide resulting from depression, as from all other mental disorders in which suicide occurs, is the background of a broken home in childhood.

Patients with self-rooted and reactive depressions may kill their loved ones before committing suicide. In these cases murder can be regarded as an extension of suicide.

Suicide may occur at any time during a schizophrenic illness. It is not uncommon in the early stages when the intelligent patient is depressed and terrified by his symptoms and believes he is becoming incurably insane. In chronic schizophrenia, suicide is more common in those patients with preservation of affective expression and depressive symptoms.

The suicide rate in western Europe is highest in old age. Depression is fairly frequent in arteriosclerotic psychoses and suicidal attempts are not uncommon. It is more frequent in organic states resulting from epilepsy, head injury, cerebral arteriosclerosis and Huntington's chorea. The estimation of the risk of suicide is not easy and even the most experienced psychiatrist can underestimate its probability.

In 1983 Ross Mitchell noted that as depression deepens psychomotor retardation saps the mind of intent and the body of organisation. It is only as the depression lessens that psychomotor retardation decreases and the risk of someone committing suicide increases. In layman's terms this simply means that an individual is more likely to commit suicide when his or her mood appears to improve as he or she will then have the energy to kill themselves.

Mood disorders such as a major depression or manic-depression may alienate relatives, friends and loved ones, and result in career or financial problems when the victim is unable to cope with the unpredictable symptoms of his or her depression or mania. Even though episodes of such illness may last only for weeks or months, the symptoms tend to recur and many victims require periodic treatment and regular maintenance medication throughout their lives. People who suffer from manic-depression are more likely to kill themselves than those with other psychological disorders.

Emile Durkheim was a sociologist rather than a psychiatrist or psychologist. In 1897 he classified suicides as being of three basic types, altruistic (unselfish), anomic (lacking in the usual social conventions) and egotistic (selfish).

In 1978 Nora Scott Kinzer stated that the old, the lonely, the childless and the unmarried are the most likely to kill themselves. She described them as 'anomic suicides', people who take their own lives because they lack *"enough norms, supporting relationships, ties, responsibilities or links to the community as a whole."* Withdrawn people who are unable to communicate may be seriously depressed, feeling guilty, reproachful or despairing. They are quite likely to kill themselves in either a fully-intended act of suicide or in a suicidal gesture that misfires and could be best described as a suicidal accident.

Many attempted suicides have been serious in intent and survival may have simply been the result of a fluke or accident. Such a victim will often repeat the suicide attempt, usually with fatal results, unless he or she is prevented from doing so. Some people may make suicide attempts for apparently trivial reasons and do so in a half-hearted man-

14

ner. They recover and forget all about it, resume living, and often have a normal expectation of life.

In 1988 Robert L. Crooks and Jean Stein wrote that there were at least eight attempted suicides for every successful suicide in the United States of America. They also noted that fifty to eighty per cent of the people who had committed suicide had previously attempted to do so.

Some people may decide on a method of suicide which might allow for the possibility of a last-minute rescue. However anyone who has a definite suicide plan in mind and has started tidying up his or her affairs is almost certainly preparing to go through with it. Teenagers often give away their treasured possessions when they are contemplating suicide.

Children are less forthcoming than teenagers or adults and may not show depression in the same way, rarely telling anyone about their condition. Even so, they are still capable of describing their thoughts and impulses and those who are attracted by the idea of death will be able, and often relieved, to talk about this preoccupation. They may talk of being "broken-up" inside and how adults seem to ignore them or are totally unaware of their presence. They will withdraw into themselves, becoming very silent, overactive or violent, and may not even cry or give any other indication that they may be considering suicide. A nine-year-old boy hanged himself, early in 1995, becoming the youngest victim ever recorded in Ireland.

On 24 January, 1996 in the *Irish Independent* Liz Allen wrote of how world-weary youngsters are turning to suicide as their only way out when they are unable to cope with the stress of modern-day life:

> Up to now, public debate about suicide has largely concentrated on adults, but teenagers and children have been left out of the picture. This is an Ireland riddled with problem children, children who are so distressed, depressed and problem-laden that they feel their only way out is by committing suicide . . . and last week, this newspaper learned of an horrific story of a 12-year-old Dublin child who committed suicide after being chastised by his mother. It was a minor incident as far as family quarrels go, the child was sent to his room after arguing with his brother over toys. Twenty minutes later, his

mother went to check on him and found him dead in his bedroom. No doubt the media and the public gets to hear of just a handful of such incidents, but the evidence clearly shows a disturbing trend whereby more children feel they are unable to cope with life.

School attendance officers are aware of a growing suicide culture amongst children. Michael Doyle, Senior Supervisor with Dublin Corporation's School Attendance Officers section is aware that "it is a feature that has arisen recently", and although there are definite reports that the incidence of young males taking their own lives is on the increase, he maintains "it is not just with one particular sex". The experts are now asking why its happening and, in the process, destroying some unfounded theories. The most prevalent theory about teenage suicide is exam pressures, but all those we talked with said there is no solid evidence to support this.

But Michael Doyle, while pointing out that he is no expert in child psychiatry, believes that there are tell-tale signs that "some of the children have had serious family problems and are living in difficult circumstances at home. Attempts are often a sign of attention seeking - a sign that the children are saying they feel insufficient for a variety of reasons".

Dr. Michael Kelleher, the director of St. Anne's Hospital, Shanakiel, Cork City, addressed the National Conference on Childhood and Death in Garbally College, Ballinasloe, County Galway, on Friday, 21 April 1995. He spoke of how the suicide rate for young males was on the increase but that there was no corresponding change in the rate for young females. The figure for male suicides in the 15 - 24 age group was eight times that of females between 1991 and 1993. He said that the suicide rate among young males in that age group was now three times what it was twenty years ago or four times that of thirty years ago. He recounted how 60 young males had died of cancer between 1991 and 1993, a period during which 161 young males had killed themselves.

In January, 1995, journalist Ann Cahill wrote that half of the young men in this 15-24 age group, the worst category for suicide, were married, while comparing a group from 1989 with a similar group from

1972.

On 10 January, 1996 Geraldine Collins in the Irish Independent conducted an interview with Dr Kelleher :

> Dr. Kelleher also warned of the need to wean young men away from the need to appear "macho", so that they can avoid the emotional *cul-de-sacs* that lead them to taking their own lives.
>
> He said the John Wayne approach of "a man's gotta do what a man's gotta do" is still predominant among young men and there is a need to give them more scope to talk about their feelings to reverse the suicide numbers. The national official figure of 400 suicides every year is underestimated by as much as 100.
>
> He said that the way we educate our young people may be a factor. Young women grow up with a greater capacity to recognise their own feelings and deal with them and women are more inclined to go for treatment if they need it. However, when men are faced with the problems of life, they feel they cannot be seen to be weak and are less inclined to seek treatment.

Widowed, separated, divorced or unmarried men are three times more likely to kill themselves than married men. Some adults may betray their suicidal intentions with an anxious tone as they paint a very dismal or depressing picture of their circumstances while others may depend too much on alcohol or drugs to carry them through life. Suicide may fit a pattern suggested by Freud that man has an instinct towards death that counterbalances his drive for self-preservation and reproduction.

A. Alvarez, the author of *The Savage God. A Study of Suicide* (1971), is better qualified than most to write on the subject of self-killing. In 1961 he himself hoarded sleeping-pills to use in a suicide attempt. He "gobbled the lot" after a quarrel on Christmas Day and was brought into hospital the following day at noon, "deeply unconscious, slightly cyanosed, vomit in mouth, pulse rapid, poor volume". He had his stomach pumped out only to vomit again, which blocked his lungs and had to have an air pipe stuck down his throat in order to breathe. He was unconscious for two and a half days, slept for most of the third day, having been fed intravenously in the meantime and spent the fourth day weeping quietly and seeing everything double. With his lungs still in a bad state, he recovered to find himself in a ward for the terminally ill, at the age of thirty-one. He discharged himself, against all medical advice, on the fifth day, and returned home in poor health, feeling that he "did not want to be alive". He suffered from breathing difficulties and from sweating, chills and nightmares for another three days, but was able to join in some of the New Year's Eve festivities for a few hours.

Ten years later he wrote:

> In some way I had died. The over-intensity, the tiresome excess of sensitivity and self-consciousness, of arrogance and idealism, which came in adolescence and stayed on and on beyond their due time, like some visiting bore, had not survived the coma.

He has written several other books since then, *Life After Marriage:Scenes from Divorce*, *The Biggest Game in Town*, *Offshore: A North Sea Journey* and *Feeding the Rat: Profile of a Climber*. He is a prolific poet and had published three novels by 1991. *Day of Atonement*, his third novel, stated that he was married, with three children, and living in London.

THE WORLD OF MYTHOLOGY

- AND THE SAME OLD PROBLEMS.

The ancient texts of the early ecclesiastical scribes were a major factor in the preservation of Irish mythology, legend and folklore. In some instances an idle or bored monk may have added a mere footnote or comment to a religious manuscript but others were more diligent in recording the oral traditions of their time. *The Lebor Gabála* (Book of Invasions) was an artificial history of Ireland compiled by Christian monks and the successors of the pagan druids, the poets. This was an attempt to explore the prehistory of Ireland but there is no documentary evidence to support any record of people or events prior to the fifth century of the Christian era. The early Christians, however, had little difficulty in collecting material most of which could be traced back to their pagan forebears, especially the Celts who had invaded Ireland in the sixth century BC.

Archaeological evidence supports the presence of man in Ireland in the eighth millennium BC. The invading Celts simply utilised the existing monuments of earlier peoples by locating their own deities in the mounds and burial chambers of Neolithic and Bronze Age men. Their view of nature and the supernatural encompassed a Celtic underworld or realm of the subconscious which was inhabited by mythological creatures such as demons, goblins and mischievous spirits. They viewed their own mortal world as a realm of the conscious inhabited by humans and animals and firmly believed in an upper world or realm of the supra-conscious which was inhabited by the *Tuatha Dé Danann,* minor Celtic gods who actually predated the Celts, part of the *Siodhe* (or fairy) system of religious worship which had originated in Bronze Age times. They also had a firm belief in the paramount world of the major Celtic deities as a realm beyond their understanding. The Otherworld of Celtic mythology seems to to occupy the same space dimension as their ancient world and yet the problems their heroes faced in myth and legend are of relevance to the world of today. Time, attitudes and circumstances may change as history unfolds but people basically remain the same. The ancient Irish and their modern counterparts have a lot in common and may even share similar perspectives on suicide.

Deirdre of the Sorrows was the daughter of a story-teller named Feidhlimidh. She was reared in seclusion after Cathbadh the druid prophesied that she would be the cause of great slaughter amongst the men of Ulster. She fell in love with Naoise, one of the three sons of Usna, although Conor Mac Neasa, the King of Ulster, had declared he would marry her himself. She eloped with Naoise and his brothers but Conor had the fugitives pursued throughout the length and breadth of Ireland. The sons of Usna eluded capture and eventually sought refuge as mercenaries in Scotland. The King of Scotland, however, became inflamed with Deirdre's beauty and jealous of Naoise, and the four fugitives had to flee his court. They found safety in a remote Scottish glen or island until three notable Ulster warriors persuaded them to return to Ireland. Fergus Mac Róich, Dubhthach Daol Uladh and Cormac Conn Loingeas assured them that Conor Mac Neasa had relented and that they, Ulster's most famous heroes, would guarantee the protection of Deirdre and the sons of Usna.

Conor Mac Neasa retracted his pledge of forgiveness when the exiles returned to Eamain Mhaca (later known as Navan Fort in County Armagh) and had the sons of Usna treacherously killed by Eoghan Mac Durthacht and his band of mercenaries. Fearghus Mac Róich and his companions were furious, declared war on Ulster and ravaged the province before they departed to take up residence in the court of Queen Maeve of Connacht, Conor Mac Neasa's most implacable foe. Deirdre was forced to live with Conor for a year but she succeeded in killing herself before he could give her to another hated enemy, Eoghan Mac Durthacht, Naoise's killer. She committed suicide by dashing her head against a huge rock in a manoeuvre known as the "warrior's salmon leap".

Deirdre may have seen her own death as the only way in which she could avoid becoming the captive concubine of Eoghan Mac

Durthacht. Her lover and his brothers were dead, her allies were in exile and she had already been the victim of rape and sexual bondage at the hands of Conor Mac Neasa. Folklore views her suicide as a rational option and the accounts of her death seem to reinforce this point of view. The earliest written record of this saga, *Loinges Mac n-Uislenn* (The exile of the Sons of Uisliu), dates from the ninth century.

Queen Maeve of Connacht is best known for her devious role in the epic *Táin Bó Cúlainge* (The Cattle Raid of Cooley), the earliest manuscript of which can be dated back to the twelfth century. She was also the mother of seven sons and one daughter. Her daughter, Findabair, fell in love with one of her mother's lovers, Froech, a man who was half-human and half-otherworldly. Maeve opposed the couple's plan to wed by suggesting that Froech pay an unreasonable bride-price for Findabair, and the two parted promising to meet again. Maeve became immersed in various plots against the Ulstermen and tried to bribe Cúchulainn, the Ulster champion, by offering him her daughter.

Cúchulainn realised that Findabair was only a pawn in her mother's schemes, cut off her plaits and sent her back to her mother, Maeve. The enraged Queen then offered her daughter's hand to anyone who could defeat Cúchulainn in combat, an offer that resulted in that hero wounding and killing many besotted warriors. By then Findabair had despaired of Froech ever returning to her and had given her heart to one of her mother's enemies, Róchad, an Ulsterman. She returned to the Connacht camp after spending a night with Róchad and announced that Maeve had given her permission to wed her lover. This news created pandemonium in the camp as, unknown to Findabair, Maeve had secretly promised to marry her daughter to twelve different kings, all of whom had allied themselves to Connacht.

Seven hundred men were killed in the ensuing brawl and Findabair realised that she could no longer rely on her mother's promise to let her wed her lover. She broke down and, screaming, left the battlefield which had once been a camp. Her body was later found, caught in branches, in the still part of a nearby river. Her face was so badly scratched that it was thought that she had tried to tear it away before drowning herself. Findabair seems to have been driven to distraction and death by her mother's machinations and betrayals. Maeve is vilified in the folk memory whereas Findabair is portrayed as an innocent victim unable to withstand the stress of royal intrigue.

Tuamgraney, County Clare, derives its name from an early suicide victim, *Grian* or *Gile Gréine*, the brightness of the sun. She was a famous beauty who lived here in the long-distant past and was reared as the daughter of a now-forgotten chieftain. She was reputed to be of Otherworld origin, having been begotten by a human being on a sunbeam. When she learned of her origins she became extremely depressed and decided to drown herself in the nearby lake, now called Lough Graney in her honour. Her body was carried in a south-easterly direction by a stream flowing out of the lake, and was washed up on the edge of a wood later called Doire Gréine, Grian's wood. Her friends discovered her body and interred her in Tuaim Gréine, the tumulus or mound of Grian, an ancient tomb which can still be seen in the field in front of Roger Sherlock's home, the Old Glebe House in Tuamgraney,

Cúchulainn, Ulster's greatest hero, features prominently in the folklore, myth and legend known as the Ulster Cycle. He perished at the hands of the children of Cailitín, a warrior he had killed during the war with Connacht. As he was dying he tied himself to a pillar of stone and none of his enemies dared to approach the body until three days after his death when one of Cailitín's daughters changed herself into the shape of a crow. She landed on the stone, told her siblings that Cúchulainn was dead and her brother, Lughaidh, cut off the dead hero's head and his right hand which was still grasping a sword. The falling sword removed Lughaidh's own hand as it dropped.

Conall of the Battles avenged Cúchulainn's death by killing and beheading all of his enemies. He returned Cúchulainn's head and hand for burial with his body and displayed the heads of his friend's foes on the lawn of the latter's home in Dundealgan (Dundalk). Cúchulainn's beautiful widow, Emer, asked Conall to dig a wide grave for her husband, climbed in beside the corpse of her beloved, kissed him on the lips and willed herself to die. Emer seems to have decided to accompany Cúchulainn into the Otherworld where her husband might still have need of her passion and courage, rather than that of the Sidhe or fairy folk. She could not visualise life without him and her passive suicide was regarded as the ultimate sacrifice of a dutiful wife.

Créidh was the wife of a warrior called Marcán, and the daughter of King Gúaire of Connacht. She fell in love with a Scot, Cano Mac Gartnáin, but he refused to sleep or elope with her until he had won the kingship of Scotland. He assured her of his imminent return and left an otherworldly gift in her keeping, his own life-stone, a magic token which had to be kept safely in order to preserve his own life. On returning to meet Créidh his ship was intercepted by a small fleet under the command of Marcán's own son, Colcu. Cano fell in the ensuing battle but Créidh thought he had been killed instead of wounded. She committed suicide by dashing her head against a rock and in falling broke her lover's life-stone. Cano is said to have died from his wounds nine days later. The earliest manuscript of the saga, *Scéla Cano Meic Gartnáin* (The Story of Cano Mac Gartnáin), dates from the ninth century. Cano was a contender for the Scottish throne who died in 688 and Gúaire was King of Connacht from 655 until his death in 666.

Men of ancient Ireland seemed to display the same suicidal tendencies. One folk tale describes a friar called Seán Bráthair (Brother John) who rescued a youth who had lost his soul to the Devil's sister in a game of cards. The friar sends the youth to Hell to recover the contract he had signed and the Devil returns it on the understanding that Seán Bráthair will take the youth's place. This could only be done by embracing death and the unfortunate friar has to die either by his own, or another's, hand.

The Christian tradition espoused by Seán Bráthair would have regarded such altruistic suicide as a mortal sin. The storytellers, however, condone his action which is praised rather than condemned in folklore. The friar orders the youth to behead him with an axe but God intervenes as the fatal blow is struck and Seán Bráthair changes into a white dove that is welcomed into Heaven.

Aithirne, a poet and mystic, was considered to be one of the most acquisitive of men. He made impossible demands on his hosts and is said to have asked Eochaidh Mac Luchta, the one-eyed king of Connacht, for his remaining eye. The king complied with this request as the laws of hospitality could not be ignored and he did not want to feature in the satirical verses of the poet.

Aithirne was an articulate and learned man who could not have achieved success in his chosen profession if he were otherwise. He was, in all likelihood, a paedomorph, one who retained infantile characteristics into adulthood. His actions were those of a spoiled child (in the body of a psychotic though charismatic adult) and committed him to a course of action that is best described as suicidal. When Conor Mac Neasa, the king of Ulster, sought another woman after the death of Deirdre, his eyes settled on Luaine, a young lady of the Tuatha Dé Danann. When Aithirne heard of this he demanded that Luaine become the lover of himself and his two sons. When she refused he ridiculed her in a satire and she died of shame. Conor sought Cúchulainn's advice on how to deal with Aithirne and was told to kill the poet. The Ulster men traced Aithirne and his sons to a dwelling on the River Boyne and the self-destructive poet died when his home was set on fire.

Seanchán, another poet, may have been the one who put the various tales of the Ulster cycle together to create the saga of *Táin Bó Cúlainge*. His life spanned a period towards the end of the sixth century and the first half of the seventh. According to folklore he had been bested as a poet by a man called Marbhán who had demanded that he recite the long-lost story of the *Táin*. He set out to resurrect the saga and he and his retinue of lesser poets scoured Ireland and Scotland in a vain effort to collect the full story. St. Caillín, the founder of a monastery at Fenagh, near Ballinamore, County Leitrim, may have been Seanchán's half-brother. He told the poet that the secret of the *Táin* had been lost when Fearghus Mac Róich, a leading figure in the saga, had been buried centuries before. Seanchán and his retinue went to the grave of Fearghus and 'fasted against' the dead warrior until he appeared to them and recited the entire Táin for their benefit.

Seanchán's fast could easily have resulted in his death if the pagan hero had not returned from the Otherworld. This foolhardy fasting against a dead man can only be regarded as suicidal.

In another story, dating from the ninth century, St. Finnian of Magh Bhile (Movilla, near Newtownards, County Down) fasted against Tuán Mac Cairill in order to gain admittance to the latter's home. The saint's fast upon a noted, yet reclusive, figure such as Tuán was on a par with frivolous suicide. He placed both life and soul in jeopardy out of simple curiosity. Tuán seems to have been an early Christian version of Rip Van Winkle who had lived in Ireland from the days of the mythical Parthalán. He is said to have founded the first settlement here according to the wildly inventive *Lebor Gabála*. Dealgnat, his wife, is credited with being the first Irish woman to commit adultery and Parthalán has been recorded as the first Irishman to suffer from jealousy.

Parthalán had to flee to Greece after he had killed his parents and tried to wrest that kingdom from his brother. He is believed to have been plagued by bad luck throughout his life as he had committed the ultimate crime, kin-slaying. He established his settlement in Seán-Mhagh nEalta, the plain on which Dublin now stands, and his descendants continued to live there for over five hundred years.

Cúchulainn received his training in arms from a female warrior, Aoife, in Scotland. Unknown to him she bore his child, Conlaoch, a youth who later came to Ireland in search of his father. They met at Trácht Eise, on the Newry Estuary, but when Conlaoch refused to divulge his identity he was slain by his own father. It was only as he delivered the mortal wound that Cúchulainn realised what he had done. Conlaoch would have lived if he had told his father who he was. His refusal to do so could be regarded as either suicidal or provocation.

The *geas*, occasionally written as *geis*, was an injunction, prohibition or taboo of a magical kind, the infringement of which could lead to misfortune or death. It could also be described as a spell of obligation which had to be observed even if its violation, *col geise*, or implementation had fatal consequences. *Cuirim duine fá gheis* (or *gheasaibh*) means I place a person under an injunction (or injunctions) and these words prefaced the conditions under which our mythical heroes laboured.

Froech was once put under *geis* against having a woman in his household, fighting with Cúchulainn or swimming between November and May. The ancient kings of Ireland were protected by sacred prohibitions or *gessa* which helped them to make correct decisions and illustrated how the goddess of sovereignty imposed certain conditions on her chosen rulers. The extension of the *geis* to cover the heroes of myth and folklore came at a later date and by Early Christian times the imposition of the *geis* was represented as the privilege of a woman. If a person knew that he or she would die or be killed while keeping to the terms of his or her *geis* that person would not be termed a suicide, no matter how suicidal his or her actions were.

Conaire, the son of an otherworld man who had impregnated Conaire's mother prior to her marriage, was forbidden to kill birds, had to travel righthand-wise around Tara or lefthand-wise around Newgrange and had to spend every ninth night in Tara. He was adopted by Eterscéile, was fostered on the Curragh of Kildare, and walked naked to Tara on the advice of a bird that had taken the shape of a man. He was crowned king of Tara but perished when he broke his geas.

Fothadh Canainne, a mythical warrior, was placed under a geas not to attend any banquet that had no "white faces" present. This was a euphemism for the heads of the dead and when he found himself at an ale-feast without a "white face" in sight he explained his predicament to Fionn Mac Cumhail. The latter solved his problem by beheading Fothadh's sister and her husband. This further aggravated a simmering feud between the two warriors and several other people were killed in the conflict that followed.

The early scribes documented the stories of their prehistoric ancestors and an examination of their records proves that there is little, if anything, new under the sun when it comes to the human condition. The social workers, professional carers, medical people and Samaritans of the modern world would be able to empathise with the problems faced by our distant ancestors. Times, conditions and man-made features may alter but the people of today harbour the same instincts as their forebears. Suicide, homicide, fratricide, matricide, crime and venality were part of everyday life.

Anorexia Nervosa is considered a modern phenomenon but stories of ancient heroes and heroines fasting to, or almost to, death are commonplace. Eithne of the Tuatha Dé Danann was insulted by a remark passed by a stranger at Brugh na Bóinne and refused to touch food or drink for seven days. Aonghas, the chieftain of the Dé Danann, persuaded her to partake of the milk of a cow imported from India by himself and Manannán, Lord of the Otherworld. Manannán came to the conclusion that the stranger's remark had driven her guardian demon away and that his place had been taken by a guardian angel. She had, in effect, become a Christian and could no longer find sustenance in the food of the Tuatha Dé Danann. She could live only on the food of a "righteous land" and Aonghus and Manannán presented her with the two cows.

Folklore claims that anyone who is born on Whit Sunday is destined to cause death or die a sudden violent death. As "a sudden violent death" is synonymous with suicide, this old tradition could be associated with self-killing. Any human or animal born on that date would either kill or be killed and the only way to avert his or her fate was to ensure that the young child or animal killed another creature. Live insects or flies would be placed in a child's hand and an adult would close the infant's fingers over the sacrificial creature in order to kill it. This killing would then nullify the foretold fate and the child could lead a normal life. Horses, cows, dogs and other animals born on Whit Sunday underwent a similar ritual in order to avoid fulfilment of their predestined fate. The term *Cíngcíseach,* Pentecostal-born, from *Cíngcíseach,* Pentecost, was applied to animals or humans.

The Celts were part of a prehistoric movement which had dispersed the Indo-European peoples throughout Asia and Europe and they had emerged as one of the most important peoples in the first millennium before the birth of Christ. Celtic was a linguistic rather than a generic term initially and was applied to some of those people who shared a common language, similar religious beliefs and a common social structure. By 500 BC the Celts were in occupation of that part of central Europe which later comprised the modern states of Austria, Czechoslovakia, southern Germany, Hungary and Switzerland. They had penetrated into Spain before 450 BC and from there they had migrated northwards to Ireland. The Mediterranean peoples had encountered the Celts in the fifth and sixth centuries BC' Rome had been sacked by them in 390 BC, and they had established the state of Galatia in Asia Minor in the third century BC.

Celtic mercenaries enrolled in the army of Ptolemy II, Pharaoh of Egypt from 283 to 246 BC. They helped him to defeat his brother Magas about 259 BC but before he could consolidate his victory the corps of 4,000 Celtic warriors mutinied. The Egyptians suppressed the mutiny and imprisoned the Celts on an island in the Sebennytic arm of the Nile. The prisoners perished either by starvation or some form of ritual suicide. Self-killing seems to have been considered a rational alternative to the Celts. A small bronze statue in a Naples museum represents the suicide of Brennos, a Celtic leader who had raided the Temple of Delph in 279 BC. Aneroestus killed himself in 225 BC when he and two other Celtic kings, Concolitanus and Britomarus, were defeated by two Roman armies near Cape Telamon (Italy).

A MORTAL SIN

- AND THE LAND OF SAINT AND SCHOLARS.

An elderly mission priest is said to have exhorted his Donegal congregation to avail of the confessional. "You won't shock or embarrass me," he is quoted as saying, "because there isn't a sin in this world that hasn't been confessed to me at some time or another!" As he warmed to his theme he offered a ten pound reward to anyone present who could name a sin that had never been confessed to him. He was silenced when somebody asked, "What about suicide, Father?"

Suicide was sometimes known as the unconfessed sin for obvious reasons but it could also be a sin in another sense as both church and state were reluctant to discuss it until recently. Coroners, for several reasons, mainly legal, will simply give a clinical description of how somebody met his or her death without actually stating that he or she had committed suicide. It is considered a grave sin if committed with a clear mind or with the intention of giving scandal but the new universal Catechism of the Catholic Church suggests that relatives should not despair of the eternal salvation of people who have killed themselves.

The Christian Churches now offer the victim some hope of survival or redemption in the afterlife but still condemn the act itself as a sin and refused Christian burial to those who had taken their own lives. In the not so distant past they would not allow the interment of suicide victims in consecrated ground, even if that ground was owned by local authorities, and were reluctant to mention the subject of suicide in homilies until recent times.

Dr. Dermot Clifford devoted his Lenten Pastoral Letter to suicide in 1990 and Bishop Edward Daly of Derry followed suit in 1993. But many of the Christian clergy are still unsure of how to handle this matter. Suicide is still regarded by the Catholic Church as interfering with the prerogative of God.

The Catechism of the Catholic Church offers some faint hope of salvation to suicides:

> Grave psychological disturbances, anguish or grave fear of hardship, suffering or torture can diminish the responsibility of the one committing suicide.

> We should not despair of the eternal salvation of persons who have taken their their own lives. By ways known to him alone can God provide the opportunity for salutary repentance. The church prays for persons who have taken their own lives.

The Catholic Church, like other Christian churches, no longer opposes the burial of suicides in consecrated ground. It still treats the act of suicide as a serious sin and is quite definite in its condemnation:

> Everyone is responsible for his life before God who has given it to him. It is God who remains the sovereign Master of life. We are obliged to accept life gratefully and preserve it for honour and the salvation of our souls. We are stewards, not owners, of the life God has entrusted to us. It is not ours to dispose of.

> Suicide contradicts the natural inclination of the human being to preserve and perpetuate his life. It is gravely contrary to the just love of life. It likewise offends love of neighbour because it unjustly breaks the tie of solidarity with family, nation and other human societies to which we continue to have obligations. Suicide is contrary to love for the living God.

> If suicide is committed with the intention of setting an example, especially to the young, it also takes on the gravity of scandal. Voluntary co-operation in suicide is contrary to the moral law."

The Catholic Church teaches that suicide is forbidden by the Fifth Commandment, and "is contrary to justice, hope and charity".

The ancient Romans regarded suicide without fear or revulsion. They felt that it did not conflict with their principles or way of life and considered that death by suicide was a rational way to die as it was not an offence against either religion or morals. Slaves and soldiers, however, belonged to their masters or the state and it was a crime for either to commit suicide. It was also an offence for criminals to kill themselves to avoid trials which would result in the forfeiture of their estates, and the casual disregard for life in imperial Rome resulted in rational suicide being regarded as an antidote to the more general bloodlust.

The early Christians assimilated the Roman attitudes to death and suicide and accepted martyrdom with a willingness that made it as much their own creation as the Roman persecutions. They showed the same indifference to death as their tormentors. Their view of Heaven made life itself unimportant. Martyrdom promised a life of eternal bliss and redemption from sin and people yearned to be martyrs.

The Donatists, a fanatical sect with an extreme lust for martyrdom, were condemned as heretics by the early Church. Members of this fourth and fifth century cult had a horror of life. They tried to procure their own deaths by provocation, and committed suicide when they were unable to find martyrdom, usually by throwing themselves over cliffs or precipices.

St. Augustine argued that the suicidal mania of the would-be martyrs was "a detestable and damnable wickedness" and recognised the dilemma under Christian teaching which made it logical for converts or the newly-baptised to kill themselves rather than sin. He formulated the argument that any man who killed himself was breaking the Fifth Commandment.

The Council of Orleans met in 533 and condemned suicide as a serious crime by the formulation of a law that denied Christian burial to anyone who committed suicide while accused of a crime. In 562 the Council of Braga refused funeral rites to all suicides, regardless of class or social position, and in the year 693 the Council of Toledo decreed that anyone who attempted suicide would be excommunicated.

St. Bruno called suicides "martyrs for Satan" in the eleventh century. St. Thomas Aquinas described suicide as a "mortal sin against God, the giver of life", during the thirteenth century, and Canon Law carried the Church's condemnation of self-killing into modern times. The teaching of the Catholic Church is contained in the Declaration on Euthanasia which was published on 5 May, 1980. This clearly states, in Article 3:

> Intentionally causing one's own death, or suicide, is therefore equally as wrong as murder and such an action on the part of a person is to be considered as a rejection of God's sovereignty and loving plan. Furthermore, suicide is also often a refusal of love for self, the denial of the natural instinct to live, a flight from the duties of justice and charity owed to one's neighbour, to various communities or to the whole society - although, as is generally recognised, at times there are psychological factors present that can diminish responsibility or even completely remove it.

Christian burial was given to suicide victims when coroners returned verdicts stating that people had killed themselves while "of disturbed mind". Such verdicts circumvented canon and secular law and suggested that the victims could not be held responsible for their own actions or deaths. This soothed the sensibilities of officiating clergymen. Many suicide victims were refused Christian burial in the conventional graveyards or were buried without Christian burial rites either in a killeen or in a remote part of a graveyard.

Killeen or *kyle* is a derivative of the word *cillín*, meaning a churchyard set apart for infants, or *cillíneach*, a place set apart for the burial of unbaptised children, who were usually buried at night, between sunset and sunrise. *Ceallúrach* and *callatrach* are variant forms of the same words and all owe their origin to the Latin word *cella*, a church or graveyard. These unofficial graveyards often appear on the ordnance survey maps as "children's burial grounds" or "disused burial grounds". They appear to date from about the fifth century onwards and were reserved for the burial of unbaptised children, Jews, pedlars, strangers, pregnant women and suicides. They seem to have remained in use for the burial of stillborn or unbaptised children into the 1950s in many parts of Ireland, particularly the western counties.

The practice of burying unbaptised children, dwarves, Jews, pedlars, paupers and strangers in killeens can be dated back 1,500 years or more. The bodies of strangers, found by the road, especially in famine times, were usually interred in the nearest killeen as the impoverished locals rarely had the means to transport them elsewhere. I cannot remember where I first heard of suicide victims being buried as "strangers" in killeens as I was not researching suicide at the time, but it may have been in the barony of Dunmore, in east Galway, an area in which over fifty such burial grounds still exist. Gerry O'Leary found the same euphemism in use in County Kerry and since then I have heard of the practice throughout Clare, Limerick, Roscommon, Sligo, Leitrim, Tipperary, Mayo and Donegal. A suicide victim could be buried as a stranger outside of his or her own home area and friends and relatives would have the comfort of knowing where their loved one was interred.

In East Clare the burial of suicides took place at night, usually with no women present. Untreated post-natal depression seems to have been the principal reason for a spate of female suicides in south-east Clare in the late 1950s and 1960s and I wondered if post-natal depression was one of the reasons why women were not allowed to attend the killeen interments in the regions around Clonlara and Tuamgraney!

"Found lost" was a Galway term for the dead bodies recovered from the Corrib or the sea. The local authorities buried these supposedly unknown suicide victims in the Plot of the Angels, a killeen now enclosed within the boundaries of the old cemetery at Rahoon. Many Galwegians refused to identify the "found lost" because they knew that the dead would receive burial with some measure of dignity in the Plot of the Angels. If they identified the "found lost" and claimed their dead relatives or friends they would then encounter major difficulties, especially in trying to persuade clergymen to permit burial in consecrated ground.

Unbaptised children were buried in killeens rather than in consecrated ground as their souls were believed to inhabit a place or state of rest called Limbo. This was said to be located at *Sruth Orthulain* (possibly the River Jordan) and the existence of such an otherworld was an accepted part of Catholic teaching until recent times. Limbo has now been abolished by the Vatican but the *Catechism of the Catholic Church* (1994) offers cold comfort to grieving parents:

As regards children who have died without baptism, the Church can only entrust them to the mercy of God, as she does in her funeral rites for them. Indeed, the great mercy of God who desire that all men should be saved, and Jesus' tenderness toward children which caused him to say "Let the children come to me, do not hinder them", allow us to hope that there is a way of salvation for children who have died without baptism.

The fairy lore of south-east England once claimed that unbaptised and pagan children turned into pixies or piskies when they died. In Russia, Scotland and other parts of England the souls of stillborn and unbaptised children were said to have animated the bodies of elves bearing these phosphorescent lights known as the 'Will o' the Wisp'. The Irish fairies seemed to have added to their number by taking unbaptised children into their ranks and, occasionally, kidnapping the children of mothers who had neglected to say their prayers. They were, themselves, barred from Heaven but, according to the folklore of Donegal and Galway, they were allowed to escort the souls of the human dead to its gates. The folklore of County Down, however, stated that the spirits of unbaptised children and suicides always returned to the spot where they had died and that the suicides were condemned to re-enact the way in which they had killed themselves.

The burials of suicides seem to have been similar to those of unbaptised children. Old Kilcash graveyard is located to the west of Kilcash Castle, almost seven miles north-west of Carrick-on-Suir. The folklore of this region stated that the graves of some suicides were marked by boulders outside the churchyard walls. I was able to locate only one boulder, a large erratic, on the northern side of the graveyard. This may mark the site of a burial and can be seen outside the inner gate of the cemetery. Local people informed me of how large stones in the vicinity of the churchyard had been moved in recent times and that these may have marked the graves of people who had served in the nearby castle.

Mairtín Ó Cadhain (1907-1970) published *Cré na Cille,* the earth of the churchyard, in 1949. This fictional work epitomised the non-Christian ideas prevalent in the older Irish culture as the dead of a parish held detailed conversations with one another from their graves.

In some regions the notion of segregating the sexes in church was also carried into effect in death. There were separate graveyards for men and women in places like Omey Island, off County Galway, Carrickmore in County Tyrone, the island of Inishmurray, off County Sligo, and elsewhere. The dead were regarded as if they were still living people but suicides were rarely mentioned, possibly because most were by then being buried outside the boundary walls of the Christian graveyards. The Established Church and the Roman Catholic Church tried to stamp out certain aspects associated with the traditional wakes but many of the customs and traditions survive into modern times.

In the archives of the Irish Folklore Department at University College Dublin there is a piece of folklore that seems to reflect the Church's teaching on suicide. According to the story, the other dead in a graveyard would turn in their graves and lie face-down in disgust if a suicide was buried in their consecrated ground.

The clergy are not immune from suicide. A suicide plot containing the body of a student priest who had killed himself can be seen outside the boundary of the seminary graveyard in Maynooth, County Kildare. Some of his erstwhile companions, priests and nuns who had served in the monastery and a few locals are interred in the graveyard. According to the folklore of the region there was a "suicide room" in the college. This had to be closed because several students had attempted to kill themselves after sleeping there. The college authorities are said to have removed the corridor wall and turned the room into an alcove.

In a footnote to his chapter on euthanasia in *Morals, Law and Life* Cathal B. Daly wrote:

> There is a significant negative correlation, noted by all observers, between religious belief and the suicide rate. Catholics are notably less prone to suicide than Protestants (Jews are less prone than either) . . . Durkheim seeks to explain this correlation by saying that religion affects suicide-rates, not because of its doctrine, but because it provides the individual with social solidarity and cohesion (- and forbids him to think!). Catholicism is more anti-suicidogenic because its social structure is tighter and firmer (- and its pro-

hibition of thought more effective!) . . . Durkheim's anxiety was that Christianity is on the way out anyhow (since this is almost the twentieth century). How, then, can society defend itself against suicide without the help of religious myths? He tries to find in the objective reality and needs of society grounds for the unqualified moral condemnation of suicide. Then he looks to social reform and social security to provide the psychological defences against suicide. His hopes are scarcely borne out by contemporary experience.

SUICIDE

THE IRISH EXPERIENCE

SIGNS OF THE TIMES

Dr. Michael Kelleher, Cork, is regarded as one of Ireland's leading experts on suicide. He has established a government funded suicide research foundation, as he believes that a co-ordinated national approach to the problem might help to reverse current trends. He told Brenda Power of *The Sunday Tribune*, in an interview published on 30 April, 1995, that increasing openness in the discussion of suicide might be counterproductive among young and vulnerable people. He did not believe in the recent Samaritan video and Outreach programme for schools which specifically discuss suicide as a response to youthful trauma and felt it would be more helpful to talk about stress and the methods of dealing with it.

Samaritan speakers, however, have discovered that their Outreach programme has been particularly effective amongst the young and that school children often form their most perceptive audiences. After any initial shyness has been dispelled the Samaritan speakers are subjected to the most searching and penetrating of questions, on virtually any subject, particularly suicide. Michael Kelleher, on the other hand, cited American research to prove that the effect of open discussion on suicide in the schools often had "the opposite effect of what was intended". He was also quoted as saying that the distressed young person of today is more liable to consider suicide than a similar person thirty years ago. The reasons for this, he felt, were much more likely to centre on social and psychological considerations rather than on illness, mental illness or alcoholism.

Brenda Power reiterates Dr. Michael Kelleher's description of the typical suicide being a young man in his twenties or thirties whose reasons for killing himself may have more to do with social factors than with illness. She also wrote of his religious views and stated:

. . . fundamental change in religious value and commitment as one possible factor in the change. Traditional Christian values and practices accepted pain and suffering as a normal part of life, and also taught that suicide was immoral because of its inherent disregard for the sacredness of human life. Morally, he says, there is a current tendency to see suicide as a neutral act in itself, yet "all hinges", according to Dr. Kelleher, "on whether individual life is, in itself, sacred. If it is sacred, as I believe it is, then the act of suicide is inherently wrong, irrespective of its effect on others. If, on the other hand, human life is not sacred then the individual has the right to do with it as he will". These days society, rather than the individual, is blamed for suicide, he says, and unemployment is a popular culprit.

The Samaritan approach is totally non-judgmental and non-sectarian. The non-denominational National Youth Federation has a total of 35,000 members throughout the entire country, in more than 400 clubs. John Dunne, the Chief Executive of the Federation, was interviewed by Kevin Moore in *The Sunday Independent* on 3 December, 1995. He stated that there were fewer and fewer social networks that young people can turn to for help and support in times of worry and distress. The Samaritan Outreach programme to the schools seems to be the only alternative for suicidal youth.

When the case against *The Abortion Information Bill* crumbled on Friday, 12 May, 1995, the President of Ireland, Mrs. Robinson, signed the Bill into law after the Supreme Court passed its consolidating judgement. *The Abortion Information Bill* has a long title which describes it as:

An act to prescribe the conditions subject to which certain information relating to services lawfully available outside the State for the termination of pregnancies and to persons who provide such services may be given to individual women or the general public, to amend the Indecent Advertisement Act, 1889 and the Censorship of Publications Acts, 1929 to 1967, and to provide for related matters.

This Bill is now constitutional and doctors may communicate in the normal way with a doctor in an abortion clinic abroad once an appointment has been made for an abortion. The doctor may provide a patient with the names and addresses of foreign abortion clinics but is not, however, allowed to make an appointment for the abortion. The Supreme Court stated that natural law is not superior to constitutional law and allowed the X case judgement to stand (X was an underage girl who was impregnated by a man in his forties. She threatened to commit suicide if she was not allowed to travel to England for an abortion).

It referred to how the rights of women such as X are unaltered by the Bill or by the amendments on travel and information, and stated that in 1992 the people knowingly put the right to information in direct conflict with the right to life of the unborn in the Constitution. The X case judgement found that it was permissible to terminate the life of the unborn child if there was a real and substantial risk to the life of the mother. She would not have been the first pregnant girl to consider suicide. There is hardly a community in the entire country that has not been affected by the suicide of a young woman in similar circumstances.

The writer Kate Hill has documented how British women's lives changed radically during the 1960s and 1970s. More women entered the work force and the better-qualified young women were better able to compete with young men in the labour market. As they gained more control over their lives, and bodies, they became less dependent on men. They eased free of the biological imperatives and politicised the emerging women's movements to demand such rights as economic equality and abortion. These 'New Woman' sexual politics entered the mainstream media culture in an effort to rehabilitate masculinity and create a new male prototype, 'New Man'. Simon Armson, Chief Executive of the Samaritans, commented, in 1993, on the increasing suicide rate in young men:

> We have this concept of the 'new man', but it seems that he is a confused man and he is not quite sure how he is supposed to behave, respond or relate in different relationships.

Kate Hill expanded on what Simon Armson said of the 'New Man':

For many he is a cosmetic creation, adapting to his changing social order by doing his share of the washing up. Real changes in male status and identity have had more tortuous effects. For "new", but also "young and vulnerable" adolescent males... empathy with women was no defence against the confusion, anxiety and guilt associated with male culpability. New Man is hardly thriving. He is committing crimes, filling the prisons, killing himself, abusing drugs in ever increasing numbers. New man appears, in many ways, a more alienated creature than his predecessors. As Angela Philips describes in *The Trouble with Boys*, more boys appear to give up on their schooling and adopt alternative sources of identity - bullying, petty crime and drug use.

A similar trend emerged in the Ireland of the 1970s and 1980s leading to the appearance of the 'New Man' and 'New Woman', a couple seemingly incompatible in life and death.

A brief look through some newspaper articles from Saturday, 12 November, 1994, to Saturday, 7 January, 1995, provides an insight into the social problems encountered in "the land of saints and scholars". This is not the Ireland of the tourist brochures but a sleazier and grimmer world in which anything can, and frequently does, happen. Has it always been like this? Is it only now we are willing to acknowledge what our society is really like? Eamon De Valera's Ireland is no more and his comely maidens have left the crossroads to solicit on city corners. This is the real Ireland, the country in which people can, and do, kill themselves.

A twenty-four-year-old Army private shot himself while on sentry duty at Collins Barracks, Arbour Hill, on 14 November. Officers heard a single shot and kicked in the locked door of a security hut where they found the young soldier lying on the floor with his weapon lying on the ground beside him. (An inquest held on Thursday, 27 April, 1995, stated that he had died as a result of a "self-inflicted injury".)

Many people engaged in male and female prostitution had traumatic childhoods that left them vulnerable to exploitation. Some are victims of abuse, most came from broken or impoverished homes or have expensive drug and alcohol habits to maintain and others are 'on the game' mainly for the money. Prostitutes can be suicidal for a multiplicity of reasons, especially fear of 'freaky' punters, pimps and gangs, fear of Gardaí and, in the cases of the discreet, fear of recognition.

A survey of teenage drinking in Dublin revealed that "the craziest drinking occurs" in the fourteen and fifteen-year-old age groups. Teenagers notice their parents using alcohol as a powerful 'social lubricant' and do not realise that it can be every bit as deadly as hard drugs. The Irish toleration of drink leads teenagers into following the adults' example and Chris Murphy, a drugs awareness counsellor, believes that children should be informed about drinking and its effects from the ages of eleven, twelve and thirteen.

Elmarie Egan, a native of Cork, attached to the University of Kent, said that abusers often needed help themselves as they may have been victims of abuse in their own youth. She was speaking at the annual conference of the Psychological Society of Ireland in Killarney and went on to say that the biggest source of referrals were parents themselves.

> This is indicative of the stress that parents themselves are suffering and the fact that they're crying out for assistance. Child abuse affects all classes in society, with unemployment and alcohol and drug abuse being contributing factors.

She went on to say that children needed to be respected and protected at all costs and stated that it was sometimes necessary to remove the abuser from the child's life. John O'Donohue, a clinical psychologist working in Dublin and Ballinasloe, told the delegates gathered at Killarney that the highest rate of suicide in Ireland was amongst the elderly. He also spoke of how the bereaved could lose the will to live after the death of a life-long partner, criticised the lack of bereavement training in medical circles and reminded his listeners of how the pain of bereavement never really went away but that the bereaved had learned to live with it. Widows visited doctors six times more often than their contemporaries whose husbands were still living and the death of a child or spouse was the main cause of stress.

John O'Donohue also spoke of how few families could withstand the strain of having one of its members murdered. Some survivors thought of suicide and others became depressed, had mental breakdowns or psychiatric problems. Alcoholism could also be a problem amongst the bereaved. The grief-stricken family members might also have to undergo the trauma of being investigated for the murder of a loved one. A family member might be charged, imprisoned and then released and the family would have to tolerate the defence of a murderer. The manner in which the legal bodies and the state dealt with the matter, the holding of autopsies, worries about how the loved one died and, sometimes, delays in burial were all equivalent to having "a second death" in the family circle.

The Irish Times of 3 December 1994 reported on the death of a Limerick man from "acute cardio-respiratory failure." He had taken high levels of the drug ecstasy. The same issue recorded the presence of Senator Mary Henry at the World Summit on AIDS in Paris, the previous day.

In Dublin women are at far greater risk of violent crime than men, a statistic that is in contrast with survey findings in the United States and Britain. *The Irish Post* of 3 December 1994 quoted researchers at Trinity College who had reported on crime levels north of the River Liffey being four times higher than those to the south. One Dubliner in ten fell victim to some form of crime each year. Dublin's senior citizens suffered substantially lower levels of personal and property crimes than any other age group and young adults in the eighteen-to-twenty-five-years-old age group bear the brunt of crimes against the person. The same issue also referred to how the body of a fifty-five-year-old Roscommon man had been left to rot in his flat and was not discovered until two weeks after his death. The suicide rate was also mentioned and John O'Donohue was quoted as saying that the elderly had the highest rate of suicide in the Republic. He attributed the cause to the sense of isolation felt by the aged who receive the least consideration from the health services. He noted that more men succeed in killing themselves but that women were more likely to attempt it. He put the ratio of both suicides and parasuicides at four to one.

In the *Independent Weekender* Maggie Butler wrote of therapy as the new religion of the 1990s, possibly because people were no "longer satisfied with what the church had to offer". She mentioned how therapy offered people an opportunity to "discover, reconnect with and express those lost parts of one's dignity".

Kathryn Hone wrote, in *The Irish Times* for Wednesday, 7 December of a thirteen-year-old French student who shot himself in front of his classmates.

The parents of a seventeen-year-old youth refuted claims of his suicide at Spike Island in *The Sunday Tribune*, on 15 December.

The *Irish Post* commented on Saturday, 10 February, 1996 how the official suicide rate for Ireland is now higher than in England and Wales. In 1992 the male suicide rate was 180 per million in Ireland while that of England and Wales was 150 per million. There was very little difference between the Irish and British female suicide rates, although the Irish rate was marginally higher.

The politics of family values merited an article in *The Irish Times* on Wednesday 4 January.1995. Communication seemed to be the biggest problem, Anne Dempsey wrote.

The Royal Ulster Constabulary were perturbed by the rise in drink-driving arrests at Christmas, according to Suzanne Breen in *The Irish Times* on 6 January. The same issue revealed how a man who committed suicide in Dublin on 27 December had phoned the Samaritans twenty-two times before killing himself. Gardaí traced the telephone numbers he had dialled, with the help of Telecom Eireann, and were able to establish that he had phoned the Samaritans and another number in south Dublin. The dead man had rented an apartment in Sandymount, Dublin, on a three-day rental, and taken possession of it on Christmas Eve. He had left a number of notes signed "Joe Kay", and was found, with his wrists cut, in a bath full of water on the morning of 27 December. One note directed his landlady to call the Gardaí, warning her not to enter the bathroom and another note contained details of his prepaid funeral arrangements. A spokesman for the

Samaritans said that all of their calls were confidential and it was not their policy to comment on who their callers were.

A volunteer from the Dublin Samaritans was interviewed by Pádraig Ó'Móráin some time before the suicide of the man known as Joe Kay. Part of the interview appeared in his column in *The Irish Times*, on Saturday, 7 January.

> If someone is finishing their life and just wants to talk to you while they die, you have to come to terms with that.

Pádraig O'Móráin commented on how this remark illustrated one of the paradoxes faced by Samaritan volunteers. They are motivated by a desire to preserve and enhance life but believe their approach must be non-directive, so that suicidal people will be prepared to talk to them. By enabling people to talk about their feelings, including suicidal intentions which they would be reluctant to discuss with anyone else, Samaritan volunteers hope that the person who telephones will come to see the situation differently. The director of the Dublin region of the Samaritans is quoted in the article:

> We don't try to talk people out of suicide . . . . That might work for a while but, at the end of the day, it won't make any difference to them.

ONE CONCEPT OF SUICIDE

- LEAVING A BEAUTIFUL BODY.

The rock music concept of suicide is to "live hard, die young and leave a beautiful body". The last part of this adage is often negated by the grisly way in which many pop stars end their own lives. The following chapter may give some indication of how few bodies remain "beautiful" when life is extinct. Sometimes the next-of-kin who have to identify the corpse become the forgotten victims of suicide. Women are generally inclined to kill themselves without maiming their bodies but men are less particular about how their bodies look as long as they manage to kill themselves in a fast and effective manner.

Antidepressants, benzodiazepines and barbiturates have been replaced by paracetamol as the most popular drug used in suicides and attempted suicides. Antidepressants prescribed for depression may take up to three weeks before they become effective and are designed to combat the physical basis of the depressive experience. They are divided into two main groups, true antidepressants and mood elevators. Suicide can terminate a depressive illness at any stage and antidepressant tablets are sometimes hoarded by patients with such eventualities in sight. Prescribed medicines account for eighty per cent of deaths from medical overdoses according to the pharmaceutical industry. They can also leave "a beautiful body" unless the intending victim overdoses in a place of concealment and his or her body is not found for a considerable time.

Paracetamol has a safe image and is freely available in grocery stores, supermarkets and local shops. It is now notorious as the drug most frequently used by suicide victims. People can accidentally take an overdose, because of paracetamol's safe image, and either die or do irreparable damage to their livers. Paracetamol poisoning accounts for over five hundred cases of liver damage each year in the Republic alone and four thousand people overdose on it annually in Britain, of which latter number five hundred die.

The majority of paracetamol overdose victims noted by St. Vincent's Hospital, Dublin, are women between the ages of sixteen to forty. They have no history of psychiatric illness and take an overdose of paracetamol to relieve themselves of misery when they are overwhelmed by an acute life crisis. People may fall asleep after taking paracetamol and believe they have recovered on waking, although feeling groggy. They resume normal living unaware of the fact that they need urgent medical attention as it takes from twenty-four to forty-eight hours for paracetamol to cause potentially fatal poisoning of the liver. The symptoms of paracetamol poisoning are nausea, abdominal pain, vomiting, low blood pressure and a feeling of confusion or drowsiness that could lead a victim to go to bed rather than to seek medical attention. If the former happens the victim will fall asleep, lapse into coma and either die or suffer from major liver damage. In some instances comatose patients have recovered consciousness to discover that they had received liver transplants in order to save their lives.

The average paracetamol overdose is usually between twenty to fifty tablets. Some victims have taken over one hundred tablets but, sometimes, as few as twelve tablets can cause severe liver damage. Paracetamol overdose is common amongst those with low suicide intent. Few have any realisation of its consequences and, more often than not, people who overdose on the drug inflict more damage on themselves than they had intended to. In 1990 the Department of Adult Psychiatry, at the Mater Hospital, noted that twenty-eight per cent of female self-poisoning victims, under the age of twenty-five, had overdosed on paracetamol.

J.P. Donleavy offered would-be suicides the following advice in *The Unexpurgated Code* (1975):

> Be neat when ending it all. It is exceedingly perverse to leave one's remains in an unlovely condition or where your corpse is likely to cause distressing nuisance. Even if it means an irritating postponement or inconvenience, always plan an appropriate time and place to kill yourself. Especially avoid any impromptu, on the spur of the

moment leavetakings involving rail tracks.

On no account can it be accepted as thoroughbred to use shot gun blasts at close range particularly upon the skull where it knocks hell out of your afterlife phosphorescence. There exists a wide range of other suitable weapons and vulnerable body sites which can achieve the desired dispatch. An elegantly embellished revolver firing straight into your heart a platinum plated bullet engraved with your armorial bearings is a stylish and dignified finishing stroke. A chaise longue is a markedly suitable setting for this type of exit.

He also offered some tongue-in-cheek advice on other methods of suicide. "If one has to jump, do so from a building in the best financial districts as it is *declassé* to jump in other areas." He advised people not to use old-fashioned poisons as it would be "ungraceful to have others view a body with distorted features" and he denounced strangling because it was the cause of "eye-bulging and ghastly grimaces." He also believed that crushing and squashing should be avoided as "they leave a diabolically shocking flatness to be scratched up".

Sylvia Plath (1932-1963), an American poetess, killed herself within three years of leaving the United States. She studied at Cambridge in 1955. There she met Ted Hughes in 1956 and they married in October of that year. The young couple visited the United States in the spring of 1957 and remained there until December 1959. Frieda, Sylvia's first child, was born on 1 April, 1960. She had a miscarriage early in 1961 and her second child, Nicholas, was born in January, 1962.

The winter of 1962/63 was a particularly harsh one and she had filed for a legal separation from her husband in the autumn of 1962. In December of that year she and the children moved into a new flat. Sylvia's last letter to her mother, on 4 April, 1963, indicated that she was adjusting to England and had "absolutely no desire ever to return to America. Not now anyway". She was enjoying life in England. Her novel, *The Bell Jar*, was published in January 1963. She wrote this under the pseudonym Victoria Lucas and it was a fictional story about a woman who learns to live with herself and the world after surviving a suicide attempt. On 4 February, 1963, she was writing optimistically of how her children needed her and of how she would spend the next few years writing in the mornings and spending her afternoons with Frieda and Nicholas. On 5 February she completed her last poem, *"Edge"*, starting with the memorable line:

> The woman is perfected. Her dead Body wears the smile of accomplishment.

Sylvia Plath gassed herself on the morning of 11 February, 1963. She left a suicide note asking whoever found her to telephone her doctor. Her baby-sitter was expected to arrive at 9.00a.m. but by the time she managed to get into the flat Sylvia was dead. The writer A.Alvarez, and others, were of the opinion that her death was a "cry for help", a suicide attempt that had gone tragically wrong. He wrote of her death and of an earlier attempt she had made in August, 1953:

> Her suicide attempt ten years earlier had been in every sense, deadly serious. She had carefully disguised the theft of the sleeping pills, left a misleading note to cover her tracks, and hidden herself in the darkest, most unused corner of a cellar, rearranging behind her the old firelogs she had disturbed, burying herself away like a skeleton in the nethermost family closet. Then she had swallowed a bottle of fifty sleeping pills. She was found late and by accident, and survived only by a miracle. The flow of life in her was too strong even for the violence she had done it. This, anyway, is her description of the act in *The Bell Jar*; there is no reason to believe it false. So she had learned the hard way the odds against successful suicide. She had learned that despair must be counterbalanced by an almost obsessional attention to detail and disguise.

Ted Hughes wrote of how it "is impossible that anyone could have been more in love with life, or more capable of happiness" than Sylvia was. In 1971 he published *Winter Trees*, a selection of nineteen poems she had composed in the last nine months of her life. One of these, "For a Fatherless Son", has three opening lines that could be applied to Sylvia's own absence:

> You will be aware of an absence, presently,
> Growing beside you, like a tree,
> A death tree, colour gone, an Australian gum tree.

SUICIDE

THE IRISH EXPERIENCE

FASTING UPON AN ENEMY

- SUICIDE AS A RATIONAL ACT.

The Irish custom of "fasting upon an enemy" to achieve justice, recover debts, enforce the law or bring someone to arbitration remained in use into Elizabethan times. *Troscud* or *troscadh*, the act of fasting, or *cealacan*, a complete fast, seem to have been recognised as an effective social mechanism from medieval times. A complainant would starve himself on the doorstep of a defendant from whom he was seeking redress until his complaint was resolved or until he died. As hospitality and generosity were so highly esteemed in ancient Ireland it was considered particularly repugnant to have a complainant starve himself to death outside one's doorway. The defendant was not alone in breach of the laws of hospitality in such instances but was held responsible for the complainant's death and had to compensate the dead man's family. Early Indian law recognised "legal fasting" as a means of obtaining redress or justice and it remained in use in Nepal into the late nineteenth century.

The people of ancient Ireland were governed under the Brehon Laws and the crime of *fionghal* or *fingal*, kin-slaying, was considered horrendous as it struck at the very root of a society based on the clan, *clann* or family system. Men who killed their kin could not atone for their offence by payment, other relatives could not put the killer to death as they themselves would be guilty of fingal, and any fort in which such a crime had been committed could be destroyed with impunity. Suicide was classed as kin-slaying under the Brehon Laws and the victim was described as a *kin-slayer* or *fingalach*.

The Brehon Laws formed a native legal system that existed in its entirety before the ninth century. They were only partly displaced by the Viking, Anglo-Norman and, later, English settlements, and was finally abolished in the early seventeenth century. A more proper designation is *Fenechas*, the law of the *Feine* or *Fene,* the free land-tillers.

59

As judgements were delivered by a brehon, from the word *breitheamh* or *breitheamhan*, meaning a judge, they became known as the Brehon Laws. These laws also enshrined a unique method of obtaining redress, the practice of fasting upon an enemy. Any man who felt he had been wronged went to the house of his adversary and brought witnesses with him. He then went on hunger strike against his enemy and if he perished in the process the witnesses would make sure that his family were compensated by whoever allowed him to die. This custom was common to both India and Ireland, in ancient and modern times and was not regarded as suicide in the modern sense. Anyone who died "fasting upon an enemy" was not considered guilty of fingalach.

Fionghal, the slaughter of a fellow-tribesman or relative, was also applied to the killing of one's own self under the Brehon Laws. *Féinmharú* and *féinídiú* seem to be of fairly recent construction based on *féin,* meaning self, *mharú* meaning killing and *ídiú* a modern variant of *íughadh*, the act of destroying, consuming, wearing away or an evil fate. *Chuir sé lámh ina bhás féin*, he put hand on his own death, may be a simple hibernicism of an English term.

John Daly (1846-1916), an old Fenian and a leader of the Irish Republican Brotherhood, was arrested in Birkenhead on 11 April 1884. He was charged with carrying explosives, sentenced to life imprisonment but was released after serving twelve and a half years behind bars. He was the first Irish political prisoner of modern times to use the hunger strike weapon against the British. Daly was elected as a Member of Parliament for Limerick while in Portland Prison and owed his subsequent release to public agitation. Fergus Kelly, author of A Guide to Early Irish Law (1988), noted that the use of fasting for political purposes was quite distinct from "legal fasting" or "fasting upon an enemy". Both, however, were used to exert moral pressure on more powerful adversaries.

Suffragettes emulated his example in later years by going on hunger strike in Mountjoy Gaol. This won a concession from the Viceroy, Lord Aberdeen, who stated that they would be classed as first-class misdemeanants rather than criminals.

Hanna Sheehy-Skeffington (1877-1946) was the daughter of David Sheehy of Loughmore, County Tipperary. She was a graduate of the Royal University of Ireland, an examining body with power to award degress. It was a university with a staff, but no student body and continued to operate until the National University of Ireland and the Queen's University of Belfast were established in 1908. Hanna become the founder of the Women Graduates' Association in 1901 and of the Irish Women's Franchise League, an Irish suffrage movement, in 1908. She was one of four Irish suffragettes who went on hunger strike on 15 August, 1912, in sympathy with some of their English colleagues who had also been imprisoned in Mountjoy Gaol, Dublin. "Hunger-strike was then a new weapon - we were the first to try it out in Ireland", Hanna Sheehy-Skeffington wrote at a much later date, "had we but known, we were the pioneers in a long line".

The Irish suffragettes were released five days later, mainly because they had served the full terms to which they had been sentenced. The English women were not so lucky, however. Three members of the Women's Social and Political Union had travelled to Dublin, unknown to the Irish suffragettes, to disrupt the British Prime Minister's state visit to Dublin on 18 July, 1912. They threw a hatchet into his carriage, missing Henry Herbert Asquith (1852-1928) but grazing his travelling companion, John Redmond (1856-1918). They escaped and later attempted to burn down the city's Theatre Royal where the prime minister intended to speak. There were riots throughout Dublin as the people of the city showed their disapproval of all suffrage activities and vented their spleen on women associated with the movement. Four Irish suffragettes were imprisoned for breaking windows and the three English women were captured, tried and sentenced around the same time. Mary Leigh and Gladys Evans were sentenced to five years penal servitude and Lizzie Baker was sentenced to seven months' hard labour. The trio went on hunger strike when the authorities refused to acknowledge them as political prisoners.

The strike commenced on 14 August, 1912, but Lizzie Baker was given early release on health grounds. Mary Leigh and Gladys Evans were forcibly fed from 20 August, 1912, the former being threatened with confinement in a mental asylum. It was once proposed that the two should be transferred to the prison hospital in Tullamore's female prison. They were eventually released on convict licence (similar to parole) and hospitalised. Gladys Evans was forcibly fed for fifty-eight days while Mary Leigh had endured forty-six days of the treatment. They were the only suffragette prisoners who were subjected to force-feeding in Irish prisons even though thirty-five suffragettes were imprisoned between 1912 and August of 1914. Their victory was over-shadowed in the following years by other hunger-strikers such as James Connolly (1868-1916), in 1913 and Francis Sheehy-Skeffington (1878-1916), Hanna's husband, in 1915. Both men had been threatened with, but not subjected to, force-feeding.

Thomas Ashe (1885-1917) was a teacher, revolutionary and Republican propagandist. He played a major role in the Easter Rebellion, was imprisoned in the aftermath of the abortive rising and subsequently released, but was jailed, again, in 1917. He organised a hunger-strike amongst Sinn Féin prisoners in Mountjoy Gaol on 20 September and was forcibly fed by the prison authorities. He was transferred to the nearby Mater Hospital on 25 September 1917 where he died at 9.50p.m., almost four hours after his admission. He spoke to two Capuchin friars, Father Albert and Father Augustus, at about 9.00p.m. "I was splendid this morning," he said, "until forcibly fed. The forcible feeding upset me completely". Thomas Ashe was the first Republican to die on hunger strike in Ireland.

Terence MacSwiney (1879-1920), Lord Mayor of Cork, was arrested under the Defence of the Realm Act on 12 August 1920. He was trans-ferred to Brixton Prison three days after he had gone on hunger strike, one that resulted in his death seventy-four days later, on 25 October 1920. "It is not those who can inflict the most, but those that can suffer the most who will conquer", he had said at his inauguration ceremony on 30 March 1920. He was a poet and playwright, as well as a Republican and politician.

Joseph Murphy, who had gone on hunger strike with Terence MacSwiney, died in Cork Jail, also on 25 October 1920, after fasting for seventy-four days. He was one of several men arrested with Terence MacSwiney at a brigade meeting of the I.R.A. in Cork. When the latter declared he would go on hunger-strike as a protest against "the incessant arrest of public representatives" most of those arrested with him declared that they were willing to do likewise. Joseph Kenny and Michael Fitzgerald died in the protest which was abandoned at the request of Arthur Griffith, Acting President of the Republic. Ten men survived on this particular occasion: Michael Burke, John Crowley, Peter Crowley, Thomas Donovan, Seán Hennessy, Joseph Kelly, Connie Neenan, Michael O'Reilly, John Power and Christopher Upton.

In 1972 Billy McKee and Prionsias McAirt directed a hunger-strike in order to achieve "political status" for Republican prisoners in Crumlin Road Jail, Belfast. Six men went on hunger strike in mid-June and by the time the strike ended, toward the end of that month, over thirty Republican prisoners had joined the protest. They were granted "special category status" and brought the hungerstrike to a conclusion just as the 1972 truce commenced.

Dolours and Marion Price went on hunger strike after they were convicted of bombing the Old Bailey and Scotland Yard in 1973. They underwent force-feeding during a long, troubled well-publicised campaign that resulted in their being transferred from a prison in England to Armagh Jail, in June, 1974.

Michael Gaughan died on hunger strike in 1974, of starvation, pneumonia and complications caused by being forcibly fed and Frank Stagg died in Wakefield Prison on 12 February, 1976 after a hunger strike that lasted for sixty days. Mairead Farrell, Mary Doyle and Mairead Nugent went on hunger strike in Armagh Jail on 1 December, 1980. They had decided to do so because the British Government had restricted special category status to Republican prisoners convicted after an arbitrarily-chosen date of 1 March, 1976. Leo Green, Darkie Hughes, Raymond McCartney, Tom McFeely, Tommy McKearney, Seán McKenna and John Nixon had gone on hunger strike in the H-Blocks for the very same reason on 27 October, 1980.

On 12 November six Loyalist prisoners went on hunger strike to seek the segregation of Loyalist and Republican prisoners. Robert Adams, Thomas Andrews, Samuel Courtney, Norman Earle, Samuel McClean and William Mullan were members of the Ulster Defence Association and were also held captive in the H-Blocks where they remained on hunger-strike until 18 December, 1980 when the British Government apparently capitulated to prisoners' demands and all three groups ended their fasts.

By 27 January the situation had deteriorated once again. Bobby Sands was the commanding officer of the Republican prisoners, and plans for a second hunger strike were soon formulated. This particular "fast upon an enemy" was the most gruelling one in Irish history and those who agreed to take part in it believed they were engaged in an extremely important operation, one that could easily result in their deaths. Bobby Sands stepped down as commanding officer to take part in the hunger strike which was scheduled for commencement on 1 March 1981. He was replaced by Brendan "Bic" MacFarlane who was to oversee the entire operation and try to ensure that non-Republican mediators would be unable to interfere with the smooth running of the strike.

Bobby Sands was the first of the hunger strikers to die, on 5 May, 1981, the sixty-sixth day of his fast. By then up to seventy other Republican prisoners had volunteered to go on hunger-strike and Bobby Sands' place went to Joe McDonnell, a man who had refused to go on an earlier hunger strike because he had "too much to live for". A total of ten men died on this epic protest which ended with the death of "Red Mickey" Devine on 20 August, 1981. Kieran Doherty died on 2 August 1981, after fasting for seventy-three days. Martin Hudson, Frank Hughes, Kevin Lynch, Raymond McCreesh, Joe McDonnell, Tom McElwee and Patsy O'Hara died in a vain attempt to wrest the "Five Demands of the H-Block Prisoners" from the British Government.

Fr. Denis Faul, of Dungannon, is regarded in nationalist circles as the priest who persuaded the remaining hunger-strikers to abandon their fasts. He is said to have cajoled relatives into seeking medical attention for the hunger-strikers and of intervening between the fasting men and their Republican command-structure. He supported the men's demands and was in favour of their achieving special category status, but he was not willing to allow them to die on matters of principle. His attitude appears to be at variance with that of the Archbishop of Dublin, Dr. William Joseph Walsh (1841-1921), who, along with a large body of clergy, attended Thomas Ashe's funeral, on Sunday, 30 September, 1917.

Self-killing has also been considered as an alternative option by men like Theobald Wolfe Tone (1763-1798). He told his wife and friends that he would never submit to the indignity of an execution and that to die by his own hand was not suicide but simply a matter of choosing his own way of death. Wolfe Tone, writer, revolutionary and political realist is acknowledged as the father of Irish republicanism. He travelled to France in 1796 in order to organise a French invasion of Ireland advising the French to make their landing in the vicinity of Belfast, with a secondary landing in Galway Bay to secure the lands west of the Shannon. He was captured on board Admiral Bompart's flag-ship, Hoche, in Lough Swilly. Mistaken for a French officer at first he was recognised by Sir George Hill who had attended Trinity College with him.

Wolfe Tone held the rank of Chef de Brigade in the French army but was tried by court martial in Dublin and sentenced to death as a traitor. He evaded the hangman's noose by committing suicide. He cut his throat, partly severing his windpipe, on 11 November 1798, using a penknife, and died over a week later on 19 November. Dr. Benjamin Lentaigne, a French emigre, attended the dying patriot and told him that the slightest movement would kill him. "I can find words to thank you, sir", he replied, "it is the most welcome news you could give me. What should I wish to live for?"

Betsy Gray was born in Killinchy, County Down. She carried the green flag at the battle of Ballynahinch on 13 June 1798 and was one of the four hundred rebels who perished there. She fought beside her brother and her lover until they were shot down by the yeomanry. They could have escaped by riding away but preferred to fight to the death. They were not the only heroes to make such a choice.

Cathal Brugha (1874-1922), soldier and politician, was elected to the First Dail and served as President of the Assembly from January to April 1919. He then became Minister for National Defence, a position he retained in the Second Dail. He was bitterly opposed to the Treaty and fought on the Republican side during the Civil War, being fatally wounded during the siege of the Four Courts. By Tuesday 4 June 1922, all of the Republican outposts had been evacuated and were on fire with the exception of the Granville Hotel which was held by Cathal Brugha, seventeen men and three women, Cathleen Barry, Linda Kearns and Mary MacSwiney. Cathal Brugha had the option of escaping or surrendering. He ordered his company to surrender on Wednesday morning which they did, with the exception of Linda Kearns and Dr. J.P. Brennan who remained behind, having guessed his intention. Later that morning he made a heroic last stand and rushed at the Free State forces, raising a revolver in each hand. He was fatally wounded and died two days later. Charles William St. John Burgess changed his name to Cathal Brugha soon after he joined the Gaelic League in 1899. He seems to have been reared in the old Irish tradition that lauded the ideal of dying for one's country. This was at variance with the terrorist adage of making sure that the other man, the enemy, died for his.

Patrick O'Brien (1820-1835) was a victim of altruistic suicide as he went to his death willingly in order to save his companions. He was one of four sailors who were killed and eaten by their shipmates after the Limerick ship *Francis Spaight* was upended in a snowstorm in 1835. All of the food supplies were lost, three of the eighteen-man crew were drowned, and the crippled ship was only kept afloat by its cargo of timber. The survivors agreed that they could only survive by cannibalism. Each one declared himself willing to die in order to feed his comrades, and the crew drew lots to decide on who was to die. Eleven men, including the captain, were rescued by the brig *Agenora* on 23 December, 1835. They were later tried for murder and acquitted, as Patrick O'Brien and his fellow victims had volunteered to die so that the others could live.

Suicide has to be considered as a rational preference when it is chosen as an alternative to dying painfully from an incurable disease. Someone who is physically sick, with little hope of a cure and unable to play any role in community activity may very well kill himself or herself rather than become a burden in their own, or society's, eyes. The risk of a self-destructive act can be higher at certain times during the development of a progressive illness as people in such circumstances can become seriously depressed. Anyone may think of committing suicide at any time. Some may reconsider the proposal and reject it, but others may regard it as a release from an unbearable emotional or physical pain.

A painful physical illness, coupled with long periods of disturbed sleep, may lead someone into considering suicide. It is by no means unusual for people with a serious or even fatal sickness to take their own lives as their limited future appears to contain only misery and the anticipation of death. James A. Harden-Hickey (1854-1898) the author of *Euthanasia: The Aesthetics of Suicide* (1894), believed in euthanasia and promoted the idea that suicide was a privilege to which anyone could aspire. His book gave details of eighty-eight fatal poisons and fifty-one lethal instruments all of which could be used in self-killing. He was a noted eccentric of Irish and French extraction, one of the old Wild Geese families. A Papal baron by 1878 he was married twice, secondly to Anna, an heiress of the Standard Oil family, Flagler. He had a ranch in Mexico and proclaimed himself the self-appointed king of what he described as the "independent state" of Trinidad, an island of about sixty square miles, 700 miles off the coast of Brazil. He announced his intention of founding the nation of Trinidad in 1893 but was thwarted by the British occupation of the island in 1895. Britain ceded Trinidad to the Brazilians in 1896 and James A. Harden-Hickie never realised his grandiose ambitions. In 1898 he committed suicide by taking an overdose of morphine, a relatively simple and painless way to die.

The Voluntary Euthanasia Society was founded in England sixty years ago in order to promote one's human right to a gentle and easy death. The implementation of such a requirement runs contrary to the idea that dying should be left to nature and an assisted suicide is in breach of the current laws of both Ireland and England. The Catholic Church finds euthanasia morally unacceptable but condones the discontinuation of "medical procedures that are burdensome, dangerous, extraordinary or disproportionate to the expected outcome". The Church teaches that the sick and handicapped should be helped to lead lives that are as normal as possible and any act or omission which causes death, in order to eliminate suffering, constitutes a murder.

> Even if death is thought imminent, the ordinary care owed to a sick person cannot be legitimately interrupted. The use of painkillers to alleviate the sufferings of the dying, even at the risk of shortening their days, can be morally in conformity with human dignity if death is not willed as either an end or a means, but only foreseen and tolerated as inevitable. Palliative care is a special form of disinterested charity. As such it should be encouraged.

> *Catholic Catechism, Dublin.*

People with terminal illnesses sometimes view suicide as their only rational option. They may be too weak or too confined in their circumstances to take effective action and can only exercise their right to die with the help of another person. In 1981 Nicholas Reed temporarily changed the name of the Voluntary Euthanasia Society to EXIT and produced a booklet which told members how to kill themselves. The society was threatened with prosecution as it is a crime to aid or abet suicide in England. Nicholas Reed was later convicted of assisting suicide and of conspiracy to do so. He was sentenced to two and a half years in prison but this was reduced to eighteen months. The society resumed its former name and now has a membership of 16,000. It commissioned a series of national opinion polls throughout Britain from the 1960s onwards asking people how they would respond to the following statement:

> Some people say that the law should allow adults to receive medical help to a peaceful death if they suffer from an incurable physical illness that is intolerable to them, provided they have previously

requested such help in writing.

Half of the people questioned in the initial poll agreed with the idea of euthanasia and by 1993 almost four out of every five people (seventy-nine per cent) were of the opinion that such individuals had the right to die if they so wished. The society now confines its activities to monitoring public opinion, publicising patients' rights and lobbying for a change in the laws of England, Scotland, Wales and Northern Ireland.

The Voluntary Euthanasia Society has recorded no statistically significant difference between the responses of those who profess a religious belief and those who do not. Christians who were polled seem to agree in principle with the idea of euthanasia. Few of them referred to the sanctity of human life when it was a question of their own lives and urban folklore now suggests that some patients' deaths were hastened when people died at home.

The British Medical Association has a somewhat permissive attitude that is sometimes defined as "passive euthanasia" or "the doctrine of dual effect". This permits doctors to prescribe opiates and sedatives that will alleviate distress, possibly at the expense of shortening a patient's life. The association will not endorse active euthanasia but a recent survey by that body discovered almost one in eight doctors (twelve per cent) had complied with patients' requests to terminate intolerable lives on at least one occasion. Almost half of the doctors polled stated that they would comply with a patient's request for euthanasia if the law was changed. The Voluntary Euthanasia Society now enjoys a friendly relationship with the British Medical Association and there are pressure groups campaigning for euthanasia in thirty-one countries worldwide.

In May, 1994, a court in Oregon made a significant decision by switching the focus of the American euthanasia debate towards the patient rather than the doctor. This happened when a number of consultants, and an association named *Compassion in Dying*, brought a case before the courts in order to argue about the inequality of the law in dealing with two different groups of terminally-ill patients. One group, relying on life-sustaining medical treatment, has the right to refuse treatment and so end an intolerable life prematurely. The other group have no such option as these patients are not dependent on life-sustaining treatment. The consultants and Compassion in Dying argued that the latter group had the right to assisted suicide as the 14th Amendment of the United States Constitution guarantees equal treatment for individuals in similar circumstances. The people of Oregon passed a Death with Dignity Act (Measure 16) in November 1994. This was carried by a majority of votes but was opposed by another group which filed an injunction on its enactment. District Judge Michael Hogan issued a temporary restraining order on Thursday, 8 December, 1994.

When or if this law comes into effect the terminally-ill will be permitted to obtain lethal prescriptions from their doctors. The legal criteria will stipulate that the patient must die within a predicted period of six months, can have medical assistance if clearly requested (on specified occasions) but the lethal dose must be self-administered. Doctors will not be permitted to administer the fatal medication as only the patient has the autonomy with regard to life or death under this new legislation.

Holland is in the forefront of those countries that are opting for euthanasia. Some Dutch patients can arrange their own deaths in a legalised reporting procedure that protects the doctor from prosecution as long as he or she observes strict guidelines. The patient must draw up "a living will", a document that will direct his or her doctor to withdraw or withhold medical treatment if the patient should be in a terminal condition, permanently or minimally conscious or have irreversible brain damage. The "living will" also stipulates that the patient be kept comfortable and free of pain, especially of any pain that might be caused by the withdrawal or withholding of treatment.

Four other conditions have to be met before Dutch doctors will practise euthanasia. The doctor must be convinced that the patient is terminally ill; the patient's illness must be verified by an outside consultant, one who knows neither the patient or the doctor; the patient has to make a legal declaration, expressing his or her wish to die; and the coroner has to be informed in advance.

Dr. Henk Prins was the first Dutch doctor prosecuted for ending the life of a patient who was unable to express her own will. Although euthanasia is not legal in Holland it is permitted under certain circumstances, an anomalous area of Dutch Law. Dr. Henk Prins gave a fatal injection to a severely handicapped baby girl who was born with spina bifida and a partly-deformed brain, in March, 1993. He was formally charged with murder on Wednesday, 26 April, 1995 but the Alkmaar district court found that his action in ending the life of his young patient, Rianne, was justified. The child was in great pain, had only weeks to live and had a condition which no operation could have cured. In 1994 there were about 3,700 cases of active euthanasia in Holland.

In 1992 the Terence Higgins Trust, an AIDS charity, introduced the idea of the "living will" to Britain. This will allow an individual with an incurable illness to choose "passive euthanasia" by allowing for the withdrawal of life-sustaining medical treatment, thereby hastening death as the quality of life deteriorates.

There are conflicting opinions on euthanasia in Ireland, as elsewhere. One school of thought advocates the use of euthanasia, as an end to unnecessary suffering, while another school of thought relies on pain-killing techniques and hospice care. Dr. Dennis Donohoe, director of the chronic care division of Our Lady's Hospice in Dublin is an opponent of euthanasia. An interview in *The Irish Times*, Wednesday, 15 February, 1995 allowed him to express his feelings on the subject:

> The argument [for euthanasia] is simplistic - a patient should die a dreadful painful death or he or she should be actively killed. In a hospice, there is no need for it to be like that. The Dutch have virtually no hospice care and no doctors specifically trained in hospice or palliative care.

> In a liberal pluralistic society, it is a curious irony that in a place where there is a relatively good standard of living there is an inability to see the role of the hospice.

> If I choose to use medicine and must use increasing amounts (which could hasten death), I have no problems with that. If it causes expe-

dient death, I still have no problem. To take the converse, to deliberately end a patient's life, that is wholly opposed to the hospice message. There is a major moral difference.

Dr. Dennis Donohoe does not believe that "living wills" should be legalised here but does acknowledge that they help people to think of their own mortality. The Irish Medical Council regards euthanasia as professional misconduct and states that it is illegal in Ireland:

Where death is imminent, it is the doctor's responsibility to take care that a patient dies with dignity and with as little suffering as possible.

Dr. Paddy Leahy, a retired general practitioner in Dublin, believes that every person has a right to die with dignity when it is no longer possible for them to live in dignity. He took the opposing side to Dr. Dennis O'Donohoe in the same interview:

I think life is simply the result of sexual intercourse between people. Even if it is a gift from God, any gift can be refused or returned, even a gift from God. If your life isn't your own, what is yours . . . Euthanasia to me is a must. I am incapable of seeing unnecessary suffering and all dignity gone.. . . The living will must be legalised. I haven't yet heard a reason why there can't be a sacred contract between a patient or his or her doctor.

Dr. Paddy Leahy, now aged seventy-nine, worked at the Ballyfermot Health Clinic until his retirement in 1988. He told *The Irish Times* that he had been a vigorous campaigner for the availability of contraceptives and believed in the woman's right to choose although he, personally, considered abortion an abomination. He admitted on the RTE Radio Morning Ireland programme, on Thursday 16 March, that he had administered a lethal injection to a friend, in England, Gordon "Mac" McKelvie, in 1945. He said that he had taken part in as many as fifty cases involving euthanasia. He was also quoted as saying that he knows of many other doctors who had performed "sensible euthanasia".

Dr. Bill Tormey, a consultant chemical pathologist at Blanchardstown Hospital, informed the newspaper that he had lodged formal complaints against Dr. Leahy with the Medical Council and the Director of Public Prosecutions. At the time of writing, Peter Scully, executive director of the Human Life International group had demanded a thorough investigation into Dr. Leahy's statement on the radio programme. He described it as a punishable offence which should be treated as such. Dr. Paddy Leahy, in an interview in *The Irish Times*, on Friday, 17 March, 1995 said:

> If my life is not my life, then to whom does it belong? The state, the church, some bloody barrister with a wig on his head? What right has anyone to say "no, we're not going to let you die?"

THE LONELY FURROW

The SAD syndrome derives its name from the initials of Seasonal Affective Disorder, a term that links the suicide rate with the seasons. In 1964 Prof. Erwin Stengel noted that the rate was linked with the rhythmical biological changes of animal life. In an interview with Geraldine Collins of the Irish Independent, on 10 January, 1966, Dr. Michael Kelleher spoke of how spring and autumn are the peak times for people to suffer from psychological problems that can lead to suicide:

> It has to do with the biological changes in us as we go into a change of season, which we share with the rest of the animal kingdom. It is the opposite to the hibernation process which affects people in autumn.

People once believed that the weather influenced the suicide rate and that suicide reached its peak during the winter months. The reverse, however, seems to be true as the suicide rate reaches an annual low in November. In 1971 Alvarez wrote that the opposite is true but agreed with Prof. Stengel that the incidence of suicide was subject to a regular seasonal fluctuation. The suicide rate increases from January, to reach a peak in May or June, declines from early July onwards, and sometimes reaches a secondary, minor, peak, in autumn.

Suicide recognises no social distinctions, classes or creeds. It is not confined to either sex and spans every age group, occupation and profession; and is no respecter of persons. The decision to take one's life has been described in several accounts as lonely and agonising.

Farming is a high-risk occupation insofar as its long working hours can lead to fatigue and social isolation. The stress and strain of a farmer's life is less obvious than that of his urban counterpart but if he is in a remote part of the country he may also feel physically isolated.

Farming accidents, financial problems and broken marriages have driven many farmers to suicide. In the rural Ireland of the 1950s and 1960s many farmers did not inherit the family farms until they were in their late forties or fifties, often living lives of quiet desperation as the marriageable women left their rural communities to work in the urban areas of Ireland, Britain and the United States. Some elderly batchelors were unable to reconcile themselves to the empty lives so aptly described in J.B. Keane's books and plays like *Many Young Men of Twenty* (1961), *The Field* (1965), *Man of the Triple Name* (1984) and *Letters of a Love-Hungry Farmer* (1974). This last work introduced a new word, *chastitute*, meaning a man who has never lain down with a woman, into the English language. It's love-hungry hero, John Bosco McLane, commits suicide on the last page.

A recent report from England claims that the erosion of village life is a key factor in the large increase in the number of suicides by male farm workers. This steep rise in suicidal deaths seems to be mirrored in modern Ireland where, like their British counterparts, many members of the farming community view death as an option if things are not working in their favour. Farmers dispose of animals who are no longer of any economic use, on a regular basis. They apply a similar criterion to their own actions, especially in villages and townlands that have lost people to emigration or migration, creating areas of social isolation. Fergal Bowers in *Suicide in Ireland* (1994) mentions that farmers account for one in seven of all suicidal deaths. Dr. Niamh Nic Daeid noted how more than 400 Irish farmers committed suicide between 1982 and 1992, a figure that raised the proportion of farming suicides to a ratio of one in six of male suicides.

A few of these farmers may have borne some resemblance to J.B. Keane's characters, others may have been the progressive graduates of the agricultural colleges, and the rest came from farming backgrounds that covered a wide spectrum from the gentleman farmer to the part-timer with a few rocky acres.

A lack of human contact is now almost endemic in urban and country areas alike, but especially so in the former. Many people live alone, leading lonely lives, particularly if they have moved from small rural communities where they or their people were well known, and have resettled in urban and suburban areas where they know very few people. The old Irish custom of the *cuairt*, or visiting, has virtually died out since the advent of television in the 1960s and newcomers find it difficult to settle in insular communities where they are regarded as "blow-ins". Television sets are now the dominant features in too many Irish homes and people are more interested in watching the antics of fictional characters than in talking to one another. Someone with a problem can often find himself, or herself, with no one to talk to as his, or her, friends and relatives are watching Glenroe, Coronation Street or Fair City. Gay Byrne, Pat Kenny and Liam O Murchu may inject a little reality onto the screen but too many people are unable to differentiate between fact and fantasy. They just want to be "entertained" while real people and their problems can be "too much". People can become very reclusive in such circumstances. They see no future as they are socially isolated and are more likely to kill themselves on a first attempt. Loneliness, isolation or uprooting are key factors that drive people to suicide and some aspects of farm life may contribute towards self-killing.

Organophosphorous sheep dips are a derivative by-product of the petrol industry, produced from the same chemical sources from which nerve gas is extracted. In May, 1995, the Department of Health requested a full report from the National Drugs Advisory Board on how safe these sheep dips are. British doctors at the University of Birmingham stated that exposure to the sheep dips can effect the human brain, slow down the thinking process and render one prone to psychiatric disorders. These disorders may ultimately lead someone to take his or her life. Eoin Ryan, the Fianna Fail spokesman on ecology and urban renewal, raised the matter in Dail Eireann on 4 May, 1995. He said that prolonged exposure to organophosphates had a chronic effect on the nervous system, led to loss of concentration and memory and made sheep farmers vulnerable to psychiatric illness. As people leave the land, those who are left behind become more socially isolated while the former face a similar problem. Some individuals from either group may find themselves in suicidal situations.

The economic and social lure of native and foreign cities has eroded the traditional social network of the western seaboard over the last sixty years. In 1973 Hugh Brody wrote a book on change and decline in his composite parish of Inishkillane but has changed names and placenames to protect his sources and prevent the identification of the areas he worked in:

> Twelve of the 231 households in Inishkillane contain people suffering from mental illness associated with isolation and its accompanying depression. The nurse who comes each week to the small surgery at the back of a village bar claims that she dispenses more anti-depressants than headache tablets. Suicides, though carefully concealed in a Roman Catholic society wherever possible, are not rare. At least three have occurred in the parish over the past four years. The "mental breakdown" is becoming almost a routine part of the country life. Typically, the "mental breakdown" involves rapid and unpredictable alternation between a sobbing withdrawal and destruction of household property. As in the case of Joseph Murphy, it is invariably part of a life of ever deepening and more hopeless isolation.

One of the characters described by Brody under the alias of "Joseph" was the youngest of six children. He was born in 1915 and by 1937 only he and a sister were left in the old family home with their parents. A brother invited him to the United States but Joseph's father insisted on him remaining to work the land. They built a new house closer to the road in 1939, his sister emigrated shortly afterwards, and his father died in 1941, at the age of seventy-four. Joseph was left the home, farm and the care of his sixty-year-old mother. She died in 1963 and Joseph, who had failed to marry, was unable to cope with his lonely life. He had a 'breakdown' in 1964, talked of killing himself and was hospitalised for two months. He continued farming but became a recluse because of the stigma associated with mental illness.

In 1968 he had another breakdown when neighbours objected to him selling land to an outsider. His parish priest asked him to sell the plot to a local shopkeeper instead and Joseph's condition further deteriorated when he viewed the churchman's interference as being the ultimate symbol of rejection by his neighbours. Joseph started to call to his dead mother for help, ran out of his house, screaming, and tried to drown himself nearby. He was rescued by his cousin but told Hugh Brody in January, 1971, "I'll be dead two weeks before anyone about here'll come to the house and find me". His sense of social isolation had cut him off from the rest of the community at the age of fifty-six.

Joseph was one of too many "eligible bachelors" in parishes of the 1940s and 1950s. He had never married because his mother discouraged any matchmaking and told him that there was time enough to marry at forty. By then there were too few eligible women left in the parish as most of them had moved to the towns and cities.

Hugh Brody also wrote of a local fisherman of twenty-six who had a very tense manner that was often mistaken for shyness. The only occasions on which he seemed to become fully alive was when he was putting his life at risk. Hugh was unable to decide whether his hazardous undertakings were dangerously suicidal or a means of displacing anxiety.

Statistics regarding suicide are variable and often unreliable in countries where suicide is considered a mortal sin. In 1971 A. Alvarez, the author of *The Savage God - A Study of Suicide* wrote of how countries like Ireland and Egypt then had the lowest suicide rates in the world and compared their records with the more highly-industrialised and prosperous nations. He concluded that the latter countries had more sophisticated methods of collecting statistical information and little prejudice in dealing with suicide, and agreed on only one certain generalization, namely that "the official statistics reflect at best only a fraction of the real figures". He also repeated a story told by Mary Holland in *The Observer* during 1967.

This concerned a verdict of accidental death, returned by a legendary west of Ireland coroner, on a man who had shot himself. "Sure, he was only cleaning the muzzle of the gun with his tongue", the coroner stated. On Thursday, 26 January, 1995, the Supreme Court ruled that a coroner had exceeded his powers when he inquired into the state of mind of a man found dead from a gunshot wound to his forehead. The man died in 1988 and the coroner's jury found that death was due to "discharge of a rifle in accordance with medical evidence while the balance of his mind was disturbed". The dead man's brother was granted permission to seek an order quashing the verdict in March, 1989. Justice Blaney, giving the Supreme Court's decision, said the Galway West coroner, Ciaran MacLoughlin, should not have inquired into what gave rise to the physical injury which resulted in the man's death. This was wholly separate from the question of how death occurred.

In another, totally unrelated, case the High Court awarded damages of £35,000 against the North Western Health Board on Wednesday, 31 January, 1996. The award was made to the family of a fifty-eight year-old farmer who had killed himself on 17 December, 1989, four days after being discharged from a psychiatric hospital. The Justice described the deceased as a quiet and retiring man, a social drinker with a pleasant personality, and found the health board negligent in discharging him without adequate assessment. *The Irish Times* of Thursday, 1 February, 1996, reported on the Justice's judgement;

> . . . that as the pressures on release may be quite substantially greater than the pressures in hospital, it was necessary that the person responsible for discharge should satisfy himself that the patient was in a "firm remission".In his view, there was no evidence of any assessment that the deceased had reached a status of firm remission. A person with firm remission would be unlikely to have committed suicide within four days.

> "It has to be accepted that it could happen but, in my view, in the absence of specific evidence of deterioration it would be an unlikely event",. . . "it was unlikely that such an assessment had been carried out . . . or if conducted, it was an inadequate assessment or inadequately considered."

> He found the defendants guilty of negligence in discharging [the deceased] at a time when they knew or ought to have known that he was not in firm remission. Accordingly, he granted a decree for damages for negligence.

Another piece of urban folklore states that those who attempt suicide rarely make another attempt. In 1971 Alvarez wrote of how people who have reached crisis point often attempt suicide because their warnings have been ignored and are three times more likely to do so again after the first attempt fails. Some of those who fail to kill themselves often feel that they have "failed" in life and death and that they have "returned from the dead" to face judgment rather than sympathy. They feel that they have had a temporary release from intolerable pressure and come to the conclusion that they must try suicide again as nothing has really changed. Those who survive an attempt at suicide have fewer inhibitions in repeating the process as they have successfully got over the first psychological hurdle and often succeed in a second, or later, attempt.

Suicide has attracted some misleading fallacies over the centuries, a type of folklore that is regurgitated time and time again. Many of these fallacies have been debunked by social workers, psychiatrists and psychologists but the most misleading fallacy of all is probably the suicide victim's misconception of what will happen after his or her death. Real life rarely follows the tragic script visualised by the victim.

A modern fallacy still in vogue claims that "all real suicides leave a note." A suicide note is left by less than one in four of those who kill themselves. In many instances such notes are vague and indecipherable but some may be accusatory in tone and try to lay the blame for suicide on another.

Those who threaten to commit suicide often do so out of bravado, despair or simply to prove the seriousness of their intent. Recent studies estimate that three out of every four suicides or attempted suicides have given clear warning of their intentions but the fallacy stating that "those who threaten to kill themselves rarely do so" still persists.

The suicidal grand passion was also dismissed as a fallacy by Alvarez in 1971. He said that those who died for love usually did so by mistake. They seem to have regretted initiating the act almost immediately, and in many instances have tried to save themselves. Despite the common belief of young love being inextricably entwined with suicide he claimed that such a couple were less likely to take their own lives than older people. He stated that that the young were more impetuous in attempting suicide and were more likely to fail in their attempts. He seemed to share the opinion of Prof. Erwin Stengel that such attempts were "a cry for help" and believed that the optimism of the young would give them some hope for the future.

Eric Berne claims that romantic suicides may have entertained illusions of what will happen after death. They may visualise a sad and sentimental funeral which may not come to pass and probably believe their deaths will be a matter of deep regret to others who they believe will be sorry on hearing what happened.

Suicide is not unique to people of any race or creed but another myth would seem to indicate that the taking of one's own life might actually be a national trait. The eighteenth-century French regarded suicide as an indigenous habit in England, dubbing it the English sickness, and adopted the English word ' suicide' into their own language. The fallacy that suicide is a natural habit in any particular country has only dissolved in recent years but it is still revived on occasion.

DEADLY PLACES

Some places seem to attract more suicides than others and no region in Ireland appears to be without at least one spot long associated with self-killing. Doora Bridge, to the east of Ennis, became notorious as the site at which many Clare people ended their lives. The first bridge, known as the Iron Bridge, was constructed on Gore's Quay in 1856 and it was the scene of many suicides and attempted suicides for more than a century. The spate of suicides does not appear to have abated much since the late 1960s when the original hump-backed bridge was replaced by a modern structure, a rubbish dump was located nearby and suburbia extended eastwards.

The railway bridge, farther up the River Fergus, near Clonroad Bridge, is another spot at which people enter the water. Drehidnagower Bridge, from *Droichead na Gabhar*, the bridge of the goats, however, seems likely to acquire a similar reputation to that of Doora Bridge. People have been known to wade into the river at its side or jump into the fast-moving waters from its hump-backed parapet. The Mill Bridge, Victoria Bridge and Clonroad Bridge have also been used by suicides and parasuicides, but not to the same extent as Doora Bridge where forty-eight people were drowned over a thirty-year period. Clarecastle boatmen used to travel upriver with the tide until a dam was built below Clare Abbey in the early 1960s. They often netted more than they had bargained for in the vicinity of Doora Bridge. I have mentioned this particular bridge simply as an example of a place that has gained an unwanted notoriety for suicide over the years. It is by no means unique as there are too many such places throughout the length and breadth of Ireland.

In 1917 William and Georgina Butler Yeats spent their honeymoon in Renvyle House in North Connemara. Both of them dabbled in the occult and they held a seance in an upstairs room which had a reputation for being haunted. Oliver St. John Gogarty, Morgan Evans, a Welsh medium, and several other guests were present. The restless spirit of a young boy who had died by his own hand manifested itself to the assembled company. Oliver St. John Gogarty (1878-1957), author, patriot, poet, surgeon and wit purchased Renvyle House, built by Henry and Margaret Blake in 1811, as a summer house for his family and friends. The Irish Republican Army burned it down in 1923 but Oliver St. John Gogarty rebuilt and extended the house in the 1930s. It was badly damaged by storms in January 1991 but is now open again to the public as a hotel.

The ghost of a butcher who had committed suicide was believed to haunt number 118 Summerhill, Dublin, until that house was demolished in 1966. The house was one of three owned by the Hutton family and sold to the Dublin United Tramways Company in 1923 for conversion into flats. The ghost was believed to have been that of Patrick Conway, a butcher who cut his throat here in 1863.

A cottage in Slaney Park, Baltinglass, County Wicklow, was believed to have been haunted by a Scottish gardener. He had hanged himself having had an affair with his wife's sister, some time about 1906. This was one of several houses visited by Hans Holzer, a ghost hunter, in the 1960s. Other folklore claims that the Irish fairyland could be equated with the Limbo to which the unbaptised souls of innocents were consigned or a penitential purgatory from which they might, some day, find their way into Heaven. I have devoted a lot of space to unbaptised children in this text simply because, in death, they shared their burial grounds with those who died by suicide.

The *Irish Times* announced that the suicide rates for the counties of Louth and Meath were nine per cent higher that the national average. On Wednesday, 26 April, 1995, the newspaper reported this from a public meeting organised by the Samaritans, the previous Monday, in Drogheda. Those present were told that there was a definite link between suicide and people not having anyone to listen to them. John Dolan, the regional representative of the Samaritans, stated that 375 people had committed suicide in Ireland in 1993 and nineteen of these, all men, were from Louth and Meath. These were the deaths officially registered as suicides in that year. The actual figure may be as high as 500 a year according to Dr. Michael Kelleher, and other sources put the figure even higher than that. The meeting had been called by the Samaritans who planned on extending their service on the east coast by opening a new branch in Drogheda.

No part of Ireland can be considered immune when it comes to the question of suicide. The quays of Limerick and Galway are frequently used by people who wish to kill themselves. The stretch of the Abbey River between Baal's Bridge and Mathew Bridge in Limerick seemed to exercise a fatal attraction for the suicidal until the new Shannon Bridge opened in 1988. Part of the Corrib River in Galway, from the William O'Brien Bridge to the New Bridge or Salmon Weir Bridge, is popular with most suicides while others enter the water at Woodquay, Wolfe Tone Bridge, The Spanish Arch, Nimmo's Pier, the Eglinton Canal and Salthill.

The University of Limerick is the country's newest university but has already earned an unenviable reputation for the high rate of suicide amongst its students. Roove's Bridge, near Coachford in County Cork, is known locally as "Suicide Bridge", because thirty men, aged from eighteen to fifty, have ended their lives here over a period of twenty years. In the last six years ten men have thrown themselves off the bridge into the deep and dangerous waters of the River Lee. The spectacular Cliffs of Moher have also attracted many suicides over the centuries. The mere sight of an abandoned car in the centre's car-park often results in the Doolin Rescue Unit being called out to search the sea and cliffs.

People frequently kill themselves by jumping from cliffs or tall buildings. Adults can easily sustain fatal injuries by falling onto a hard surface from a height of twenty to thirty feet, although young children and babies have sometimes survived such falls. When somebody dives headlong onto a hard surface the skull is usually driven into the thoracic cavity, part of the trunk between the neck and abdomen. If someone lands feet-first the force of the fall will drive the victim's thigh bones up into the abdomen. Bodies that hit the ground sidelong tend to flatten out and limbs may be torn off if a body encounters projections while falling. People who jump to their deaths will often shout as they fall, an automatic reaction as their sense of self-preservation takes over, too late to save them.

The texture and composition of a body is as inert as a bag of sand. This means it cannot bounce and will remain at its point of impact on hitting a flat surface. The high-rise flats in Ballymun, Dublin, have attracted a certain notoriety in recent years because so many people have killed themselves here, by jumping to their deaths. In 1808 Hely Dutton wrote of a girl who had fallen from the top of Leamaneh Castle in the Burren. She fell a distance of about seventy feet and landed on a pig grubbing for roots at the base of the castle. She survived the fall but the impact of her landing killed the pig.

People may even travel to distant places in order to kill themselves and save relatives the grim task of identifying their bodies. Others will commit suicide in an area where their bodies can be easily found and identified. Marinas are becoming increasingly popular with those who wish to drown themselves as the bodies of those who drown in such man-made lagoons are discovered within a relatively short period. The bodies of three people who drowned in the new marina at Kilrush, County Clare, were recovered in a matter of hours. It can often take weeks to retrieve bodies from the Fergus and Shannon estuaries and there have been occasions on which bodies have never been found.

Maynooth College was founded by an Act of the Irish Parliament in 1795, thirty-four years before Catholic Emancipation was granted. The story of its "suicide room" or "ghost room" can be found in *Window on Maynooth* (1949) by Denis Meehan, *Hostage to Fortune* by Joseph O' Connor and *The Lively Ghosts of Ireland* (1967) by Hans Holzer. The room in question was located in the Junior House Buildings which were erected between 1832 and 1834. The building was named Rhetoric House, had two upper floors used for residential purposes and the haunted room was room number two on the top corridor. According to the oral tradition of the college one student killed himself in this room, possibly by cutting his throat with a razor. A second student moved into the vacant room and is said to have felt himself compelled to emulate the previous resident's example. The former in some accounts, is said to have either killed himself or saved his own life by jumping through the room's window, into Rhetoric yard. Folklore claims that the second student also killed himself and that it was a third student who jumped through the room's window to escape death, at the cost of some broken bones. These events are said to have taken place between 1842 and 1848. The student who survived this suicidal compulsion is said to have seen "a black shape" in the room. The college trustees passed a resolution on 23 October, 1860:

> That the President be authorised to convert room No. 2 on the top corridor of Rhetoric House into an Oratory of St. Joseph, and to fit up an oratory of St. Aloysius in the prayer hall of the Junior Students.

Students were refused admittance to the seminaries if there was a record of any member of their families having committed suicide and the suicidal are still barred from today's ministry. The Code of Canon Law (1984) gives a short list of those persons who are to be barred from the reception of orders. Canon 1041 finds the following "irregular for the reception of orders": one who has gravely and maliciously mutilated himself or another, or who has attempted suicide.

SUICIDES IN IRISH HISTORY

*G*reat wits are close to madness near allied, and thin partitions doth their bound divide.

Dryden.

The English poet wrote of the parallel between great minds and madness and echoes some curiosities in the Irish experience.

"Grotesque, unbelievable, bizarre and unprecedented" is a phrase coined by Charles J. Haughey, a former Taoiseach. This has been shortened and passed into popular usage as *Gubu* or *the Gubu factor*. This is the only expression one can use to describe the artful way in which William "Barnie" Shaw killed himself. He was an uncle of the famous critic, dramatist, pacifist, socialist and writer, George Bernard Shaw (1856-1950) and committed suicide out of religious fervour. His nephew wrote of how Barnie had been "an inveterate smoker" and persistent "toper" in his youth but had given up such pursuits when he devoted all of his attention to playing the ophicleide, a bass or alto key-bugle. He married a "lady of distinguished social position and great piety" late in life, to "the amazement of Dublin" and then renounced his musical career. He became a born-again Christian and was reputed to "sit with a Bible on his knees and an opera glass to his eyes, watching the ladies' bathing place in Dalkey." He became obsessed with "the fantastic imagery of the Bible" and tried to "save" his nephew from the "path to perdition" alleging that he was the Holy Ghost. He was eventually placed in a private asylum. According to G.B. Shaw every "possible weapon had been carefully removed from his reach, but his custodians reckoned without the Shavian originality. They had left him somehow within reach of a carpet-bag. He put his head into it and in a strenuous effort to decapitate or strangle himself by closing it on his neck, perished of heart failure . . . nobody's enemy but his own".

Henry Brooke Parnell (1776-1842) was apparently recovering from a deep depression when he killed himself. He was the grand-uncle of Charles Stewart Parnell. He took part in the last Irish Parliament as the member for Maryborough, now renamed Portlaoise, from 1798 to 1800, opposed the Act of Union, and was returned as a Member of Parliament for Queen's county (Laois) and Portarlington, between 1802 and 1841. He sat in a total of fourteen parliaments and served as Lord of the Treasury (1806), Secretary of War (1831-1832) and Paymaster-General of The Forces, Treasurer of the Navy and Ordnance (1835-1841). He was created Baron Congleton, of Congleton, Cheshire, on 18 August 1841. Henry Brooke Parnell was a shrewd politician and the author of History of the the Penal Laws (1808) and Financial Reform (1830). He suffered from depression and killed himself on 8 June 1842.

Hervey Redmond Morres (c. 1750-1797), 2nd Viscount Mountmorres, succeeded his cousin Sir Nicholas Morres, 9th Baronet, in 1795. He was a notable eccentric and spendthrift. He lost his paternal estates which had been held by the Morres family for over six hundred years and tried to recover his lost fortunes by abducting a young lady in the 1770s. Her friends and servants foiled his attempt to kidnap her and gave him a beating from which he never fully recovered. He never married and is said to have been so upset over "Ireland's troubles" that he committed suicide. He shot himself on 17 August 1797.

William Nicholas Keogh (1817-1878) was a judge, writer and a Member of Parliament for Athlone in 1847. He was a co-founder of the Catholic Defence Association in August 1851, possibly championing Catholic causes in order to promote his own career. He seconded the Tenant Right Bill introduced by William Sharman Crawford in 1852 and, as a member of the Independent Irish Party, was one of those responsible for the fall of Lord Derby's Conservative government. He and John Sadleir were considered renegades when they took office in Lord Aberdeen's Whig-Peelite coalition. William Keogh became Solicitor-General, rose to the rank of Attorney-General by 1855 and was appointed Judge of the Court of Common Pleas in 1857. He became notorious for his anti-nationalist remarks, as a special commissioner during the Fenian trials of the 1860s. Isaac Butt tried to have him removed from the judicial bench in 1872, and he seems to have displayed symptoms of mental instability from 1856 onwards. He committed suicide while visiting Germany in 1878.

John Sadleir (1815-1856) was an associate of William Nicholas Keogh and a member of the Irish Brigade, a group of Liberal Members of Parliament instrumental in the foundation of an extra-parliamentary body known as the Catholic Defence Association. When this group co-operated with the Tenant League to establish the Independent Irish Party John Sadleir and his colleagues had sworn that they would not accept office in Lord Aberdeen's Whig-Peelite coalition which was in power from 1852 to 1855. John Sadleir was a Member of Parliament for Carlow from 1847 to 1853, fell foul of his fellow-nationalists when he became Lord of the Treasury in December 1852, and was returned as the member for Sligo in 1853. The Encumbered Estates Acts of 1848 and 1849 allowed him to acquire various estates and establish the Tipperary Joint-Stock Bank. He lost heavily on American investments he had speculated on and embezzled £1,250,000 from the bank he had founded He was sued for false imprisonment by one of his debtors in 1854 and committed suicide as his financial depredations were about to be uncovered.

Robert Steward (1769-1822) was a Liberal who became a Conservative politician on hearing of the excesses committed during the French Revolution. He was elected to parliament in 1790 and was once considered a firm believer in electoral reform. He thought that Ireland should have the power to change its ministers at will and supported the Catholic Relief Bill of 1793. Robert became Viscount Castlereagh in 1796 and it is under this title he is best remembered in Irish history, myth and folklore. He became notorious as one of the architects of the Union of Great Britain and Ireland which came into effect on 1 January, 1801. He used bribery, corruption, threats, patronage, sinecures and titles to achieve his aims. He served as Chief Secretary for Ireland, was President of the Board of Control, and was Minister Plenipotentiary to the allied sovereigns after the defeat of Napoleon. He also played a major role at the Congress of Vienna and succeeded as 2nd Marquis of Londonderry on 8 April 1821. There followed a nervous breakdown induced by overwork, and had several bouts of depression between 1820 and 1822. He had started to act strangely in 1815 and at one stage had confessed to King George IV that he was guilty of all types of crimes. He admitted to treason and stated that he had murdered Lord Palmerston, even though Lord Palmerston was then in the same room as the king himself. King George IV asked his own doctor to attend to Robert Stewart. The doctor realised that the politician was suicidal and confiscated all of the latter's guns and razors when he called to his house in North Cray, Kent. The viscount nevertheless managed to commit suicide by cutting his throat with a pair of nail scissors and was buried in Westminster Abbey on 20 August, 1822.

Thomas Steele (1788-1848), "Honest Tom", was a staunch friend and supporter of Daniel O'Connell. He was a Protestant landlord who favoured Catholic Emancipation and the Repeal of the Act of Union. Steele was known as O'Connell's "Head Pacificator" as he was encouraged by the latter to resolve disputes that had arisen in the Repeal Association. He is commemorated by a unique monument in Ennis, County Clare, Steele's Rock. He qualified as a civil engineer at Cambridge and inherited Cullane House and demesne from his uncle and namesake but never practiced his profession. He is remembered in Clare folklore as an eccentric who dressed as an undertaker and drove a hearse carrying a coffin marked 'Repeal' to political rallies. He also experimented with diving-bells in Cullane Lake and his attempts to develop an underwater craft inspired John Philip Holland (1841-1914) to invent the submarine. He tried to commit suicide by jumping off Waterloo Bridge, in London, but was rescued from the Thames only to die a few days later as a direct result of his experience.

TERRIBLE CHOICES-

FATAL ELEMENTS

W hen people make that ultimate choice the methods they use are as diverse as the individuals that avail of them. Self-poisoning and drowning are two of the most popular methods favoured by women, while men favour hanging, drowning, self-poisoning, shooting, gassing, car-crashing and jumping.

Hanging can be a particularly gruesome way to die and in too many instances people have died slowly by strangulation rather than quickly with a snapped vertebra. Dr. Samuel Haughton (1821-1897), President of the Royal Irish Academy in 1887, was particularly interested in limb movement and muscle action and used his knowledge to render the hanging of criminals more humane. He pioneered a system of hanging, Haughton's Drop, which dislocated the joints at the junction of the vertebral column and skull to cause instantaneous death.

Andrew Carr was executed in the Richmond Bridewell, Dublin, on 28 July 1870. His head was pulled off his body and Samuel Haughton was called in to investigate what had occurred. He wrote of how the elasticity of the rope, the positioning of the knot and the length of the drop had all contributed to the beheading. He concluded by stating that it had been a merciful death but suggested that all ropes be tested before an execution and that a shorter drop should be used if any were "stiff and inelastic". His report to the Inspector for Prisons concludes with a brief history of hanging in this country:

> I would observe that the long drop has been used in Ireland from time immemorial, with the humane object of shortening the sufferings of the criminal and the records of Irish executions show that the drop has ranged from 9 feet to 16 feet. In English executions the drop ranges from 2 to 3 feet only and I am informed by Mr. Gibson, surgeon to Newgate, that during his long experience, he has known but one case in which death was rapid (case of Muller, executed for

97

the murder of Mr. Briggs on the Metropolitan Railway).

Dr. Haughton delivered a lecture on "suspension" to the Surgical Society of Ireland in December 1876. He expounded on the benefits of using a long drop of six to eight feet on a convicted prisoner, stating that it was much better than the two to three foot drop used in England, and noting that a speedier and less painful death could be achieved with a longer drop. His message and that of his contemporary, William Marwood, a hangman in England from 1874 to 1888, seems to have been acknowledged by many modern suicide victims who have hanged themselves from railway bridges and the like.

Victims of the short drop could take from fifteen to forty-five minutes to expire in Samuel Haughton's time and some recent suicide victims have taken almost as long to die. Relatives of one young man found his neck and fingers had been lacerated as he had tried, desperately, to remove the rope from around his neck.

Auto-erotic asphyxiation has often been mistaken for either homicide or suicide. This can be induced by the use of handcuffs, studded collars and leather, cloth, chain or rope bindings, and plastic bags. The sexual thrill obtained in this manner may lead someone to experiment even further and inadvertently cause his or her own death. Such a death may be dismissed as suicide, especially if the victim appears to have been hanged. A British politician killed himself, accidentally, while engaged in auto-erotic play, early in 1994.

The growth in car ownership from the late 1960s onwards has also led to an increase in its use as a method of self-destruction. Gardaí, coroners and insurance company assessors are particularly suspicious of inexplicable car crashes in which lone drivers have managed to kill themselves.

Death by car-exhaust fumes, (carbon monoxide poisoning) is an innovative method devised by suicidal motorists. This system of self-killing is used by about one in four of young males in the fifteen-to-twenty-four-year-old age group and by one in ten of British women in the same age group. The fumes from the car-exhaust are usually fed into the car by a hose-pipe or the car is driven into a sealed garage (or an enclosed space) where the fumes can overpower the driver.

Suicide by fume inhalation is regarded as painless, but lethal and leaves the body relatively undamaged, a factor that seems to appeal to women. It has started to replace overdosing as an alternative form of self-killing in Britain, since the 1970s. Death by carbon monoxide poisoning was once considered a male preserve in both Britain and Ireland but such is no longer the case. Almost as many women as men now kill themselves with these lethal fumes. Gardaí have also noted that the majority of women who use their car-exhaust fumes to such deadly effect look as if they had intended to go to parties rather than to their deaths. They wear their favourite or best clothes, don their jewellery, have their hair well groomed and have applied their make-up to perfection.

This mirrors the trend noticed by Kate Hill amongst the fifteen-to-twenty-four-year-old age group in Britain where young women are losing their preference for passive suicide. They may still kill themselves in different ways to young men but some of them are prepared to adopt the more active suicide methods of their male peers. This move towards more violent means was evident from a study of the methods used in Britain between 1968 and 1992 and leaves young women with less hope of "a second chance" at life. The most common methods of terminating life used by the young men in this age group, between 1988 and 1992 were, in descending order of popularity, hanging, car-exhaust fumes, overdosing, jumping, drowning and firearms. Other methods, including cutting of the wrists, arms or throats, the use of domestic gas, domestic or road "accidents"and illegal but active euthanasia may account for other instances of suicide.

Between 1963 and 1971, when the British changed over from poisonous coal gas to a new detoxified domestic gas, there was a corresponding fall in the suicide rate. The inhalation of coal gas accounted for half of Britain's male and female suicides in 1960.

Guns feature in a lot of male suicides, especially those of farmers.

Unfortunately the guns kept on most farms are shotguns and these leave horrendous wounds on the human body, especially when used at close range. Very few people have arms long enough to pull the trigger of a shotgun directed at their head or heart. They try to discharge the weapon by placing the stock or butt on the ground, crouching over the barrel to receive the charge and pushing the trigger down with their bare feet. On occasion people fix the gun in position on a door-jamb, chair, telegraph pole or some type of immovable object, stand in front of it and pull the trigger by jerking on a string. This can be an extremely awkward way of killing oneself and people have been known to survive such attempts only to suffer from crippling or disfiguring wounds.

Paddy Doyle and Peter Tyrrell were both detained in industrial schools [orphanages/homes where children were trained for trades], the former in St. Michael's in Cappoquin and the latter in St. Joseph's, County Cavan. Both were victims of abuse and neglect at the hands of what Paddy so feelingly calls the God Squad. The mortality rate in these schools was much higher than that in the Free State in 1929. Seventeen children, out of 6,515 in care, died in that year and in 1934 twenty-five children died out of a total of 6,420. Peter Tyrrell killed himself in 1967, a year after The Tuarim Report was published. He had had some input into this publication but did not believe the group's reassurances that matters had improved since his day. He set himself alight on Hampstead Heath, in London, and the English police were unable to establish his identity for a year. They were able to ascertain who he was by tracing the unburned corner of a postcard found in his pocket.

Paddy Doyle became permanently disabled by the age of ten. He was committed to an industrial school at the age of four, after his father had committed suicide. He was assaulted and sexually abused by his custodians and was then abandoned to begin a round of the hospitals until he wound up in St. Mary's Hospital at Cappagh. He married in 1974, at the age of twenty-three, and published *The God Squad* in 1988. Within its pages he wrote of how his mother had died from cancer of the breast in June, 1955 when he was four years of age:

...and six weeks later my father committed suicide by hanging himself from an alder tree at the back of a barn on a farm where he worked as a labourer. I was taken into court by a woman who was later described as "a sort of an aunt".

Paddy probably witnessed his father's death as he was found wandering around the farm in great distress. He was thirty-five years old before he saw a photograph of his mother as her brother, his closest living relative, did not want to talk of her or her husband, Patrick (1903-1955).

Many people familiar with the effects of institutional care, particularly Industrial Schools, will say that I have gone too easy on them. Lives have been ruined by the tyrannical rule and lack of love in such places. People have been scarred for life. Others will wonder why I bothered to delve into the past at all.

This book spans just six years of my life. There was almost consistent trauma, ranging from the death of both my parents, to the isolation of hospital wards and brain surgery. Such surgery was not just traumatic, but debilitating also . . .

It is important to point out that interspersed with this trauma were moments of great love and affection. From the gentle kiss of a young nurse to the soft hand of a caring nun. It may well be the case that these were the moments which preserved my sanity and gave me something to live for.   *Paddy Doyle*

Herman Goertz (1890-1947) had an extraordinary career in Ireland during the "Emergency" (World War II to the rest of the world). He killed himself in order to avoid imprisonment, interrogation or possible death at the hands of his wartime enemies. He was born in Lubeck, read law at Heidelberg, was decorated for his military exploits in Belgium and Russia during World War I and went to America in the 1920s. He was arrested during the Second World War and after a failed prison escape resigned to his fate and translated some of the works of W.B.Yeats in German. He was released on 11 September, 1946 when he moved to Dublin becoming secretary of the Save the German Children Fund in February, 1947 but was arrested, along with other former German internees, on 12 April, 1947. at the request of the Western Allies. He was allowed out on parole and visited the Aliens' Registration Office at Dublin Castle on 23 May, 1947. He committed suicide by taking a phial of potassium cyanide in the presence of two detectives.

Oskar Metzke (1909-1942), a German spy, captured at Castletownroche killed himself by taking cyanide of potassium on 17 December, 1942.

Gertraude Margaret Leopold was born on 3 February, 1939. She qualified as a doctor in December, 1963, and worked with Dr. Hans Herzogenrath, a man of about thirty-eight years of age, who had been divorced five years before. He suffered from depression and she later discovered that he had become a drug addict shortly after the end of the war when he had received large quantities of drugs while being treated for tuberculosis. Gertraude agreed to marry Hans before she became aware of his problem with drugs. He spoke of his tendency towards depression and mentioned how drug addiction could terminate his medical career.

The couple decided to holiday together in Ireland. A receptionist welcomed them to their Killarney hotel and noted the time of their arrival at about 5.30p.m. The two checked into room 417, hung a "do not disturb" sign on the door and spent most of their time in the room. They used room service frequently and Hans appeared to be in good form whenever they appeared, or dined, in public. However, in the privacy of their room, he spent most of the time lying on the bed in a state of depression. He told Gertraude that suicide was the best solution for both of them and she later admitted to Gardaí that his attitude began to influence her own thinking.

They had dinner in the hotel dining-room on Wednesday, 5 October, 1966 and retired to room 417 some time before 9.30. Hans brought up the question of suicide, yet again, after they had imbibed a bottle of Champagne delivered to the room. He tried to persuade Gertraude to write a suicide note and produced about twenty tablets which she identified as barbiturates, Dormopan and Doriden Forte. She swallowed the tablets at his suggestion. She woke up at some stage during the night to see Hans lying on the other twin bed breathing very heavily and tried to get up to see how he was. She picked up the telephone, with some difficulty, only to let the receiver fall out of her hand and dangle from the handset.

The night porter saw a white light in the "on" position on the hotel switchboard at about 10.45 p.m. on Thursday, 6 October. He pointed it out to someone else but she did nothing about it as she believed Hans was drunk. Gertraude fell asleep again and did not wake up again until the following morning. She had no clear memory of subsequent events but remembered knocking on the door of an adjoining bedroom and being helped back into the room by a man.

A local doctor arrived on the scene at 7.05a.m. He made a superficial examination of Hans and Gertraude and had the former conveyed to Killarney Isolation Hospital by ambulance. He accompanied Hans Herzogenrath on this journey and later returned to the hotel to collect Gertraude Leopold. Hans Herzogenrath died at 11.40a.m., despite efforts of Dr. Patrick Fuller and Dr. William O'Sullivan to save him

The Garda superintendent went into consultation with the State Solicitor in Tralee at 11.15a.m. on Saturday 8 October. The latter directed the Gardaí to obtain a warrant for the arrest of Dr. Gertraude Leopold who was charged with attempted suicide on Monday, 10 October, 1966, and remanded on bail to Killarney District Court until Tuesday, 18 October. Interpol informed the Gardaí that Hans Herzogenrath had booked only single-way tickets with his travel agents and had refused to buy return tickets even when offered a generous discount. He had given notice to the hospital saying he planned to leave on 31 December, 1966, and on 30 September announced that he was taking two weeks off to find another job.

He had lost the sight of one eye in an accident in and had a series of operations in 1963 and 1965 in a vain attempt to stop headaches. He told his mother he was tired of life but never disclosed his plans regarding travel or suicide to any of his relatives. The case was adjourned but Gertraude was remanded on bail. The Chief State Solicitor wrote to the Attorney General on 19 December, 1966, and mentioned that he had seen Gertraude's statement to the Gardaí. This had been taken, in the presence of her solicitor, on 16 December, 1966, and the Chief State Solicitor mentioned:

> The statement, although not very expansive on the accused's relationship with the deceased, strikes me as being honest and implies that she was infatuated with and dominated by the deceased and that her acceptance of the "suicide pact" was attributable to such domination.

> In the circumstances now disclosed I would not proceed with the charge before the court or prefer the more serious charge of murder if the accused gives an undertaking to return immediately to her own country and there submit to such psychiatric treatment as may be prescribed for her.

Dr. Gertraude Leopold was discharged at Killarney District Court on 3 January, 1967. The proceedings taken against her were withdrawn on the instructions of the Attorney General and she left from Cork Airport on 5 January. She was the last person to be charged with attempted suicide in Ireland.

In 1985 a Supreme Court judgement ruled that no coroner could pass a verdict of suicide in the Republic. Even though suicide was decriminalised in 1993 coroners are still confused on the issue. Under the existing law Irish coroners are unable to emulate their British counterparts and their juries who can pass verdicts of suicide once they have determined, "beyond reasonable doubt", that someone has taken his or her own life. The Central Statistics Office therefore relies on confidential Garda reports when compiling statistics on suicide and the final decision on whether or not death is classified as suicide is made by an official who is neither a coroner or a clinician. This criterion may prove to be more effective than relying on a coroner's verdict as it leaves a lower ratio of undetermined deaths on record. In the past many suicides have been misclassified and police reports are more prosaic and take "the balance of probability" into account. M.J. Kelleher, P. Corcoran, P. Keeley, H.S. Dennehy and I. O'Donnell published an article in *The Irish Medical Journal*, of January/February 1996, which advocated the further use of confidential Garda reports in order to establish a procedure that may ultimately prevent future suicides.

WHY?

THE UNANSWERED QUESTION.

W hy? That is the question many ask, searching their souls, their consciences, their memories to make sense of the suicide of someone close to them. Even the most exhaustive technical and informative texts on the subject end up with this most basic question.

> Borderlines between feeling desperate or in despair, of contemplating suicide and attempting or committing suicide, of feeling lonely or just fed up and are often wafer thin.　　　*Michael De-la-Noy*

The publication of Emile Durkheim's *Suicide: A Study in Sociology* in 1897 breached the moral and religious barriers which had shrouded the subject up to then. Subsequent publications brought the study of suicide into the realms of science and sociology and it is now viewed from a more enlightened and humane angle.

The latest research in England now seems to suggest that an inclination towards suicide may be a hereditary factor, a genetic death wish instilled at birth. Robert Matthews, a science correspondent, wrote in *The Sunday Telegraph* on 4 February, 1996 of a 'suicide gene' that may predispose some individuals towards suicide. Dr. Johnathon Evans, Professor David Nutt and their colleagues at the University of Bristol's Department of Mental Health discovered that suicidal people were deficient in a brain chemical called 5-HT:

> The enzyme that regulates 5-HT is generated by the suspect gene. How much greater is the suicide risk has yet to be quantified, but the team emphasises that the gene does not guarantee that those carrying it will eventually kill themselves.

> "There are many other influences on suicide risk, such as drinking, psychological disturbances and life stress", Professor Nutt told The Sunday Telegraph.

> . . . David Shapiro, executive secretary of the Nuffield Council on

Bioethics, said: "The real issues here are the benefits of having a test of this sort, and to what extent its results could be self-fulfilling. There must be huge questions about whether one should use this type of information." The Association of British Insurers said that it would require any applicant for life cover taking a test for suicide risk to declare the result. However, Suzanne Moore, for the ABI.stressed that there are no plans for mandatory screening before granting life cover.

. . . Scientists at the University of Illinois in Chicago have developed a blood test to identify people at high risk based on 5-HT levels. They say the probability of suicide in such cases is around 55 per cent.

Robert Matthews also mentioned how a genetic test could give early warning of those who were prone to suicide, thus saving lives. He warned of fears that the insurance companies may demand mass screenings of potential clients and refuse life cover to those with the "suicide gene", and noted how about ten people killed themselves every day in England and Wales.

The subject of suicide is still regarded with a certain amount of suspicion and prejudice, but the emphasis is now one of concern, not of censure. Suicide is now believed to be a product of social isolation and is quite often perceived as an accompaniment to modern prosperity. It is sometimes viewed as an admission of failure or, less frequently, as a dramatic gesture, and, like inflation, the suicide-rate seems to keep in line with the level of unemployment. Men seem to be more likely to kill themselves than women; the elderly seem to do it more frequently, the likelihood of suicide increasing with age; and children rarely kill themselves until they enter their teenage years, although adolescents are now killing themselves at an increased rate in Ireland, the United Kingdom and the United States.

Sr. Consillio works with addicts in the Cluain Mhuire centres. She attended a Samaritan meeting in Drogheda on Monday, 24 April, 1995, and spoke of how children find materialism has taken over and of how there is very little time for listening. She has noticed an increase in the suicide and parasuicide rates of the fifteen-to-twenty-five-year-old age group:

> In our country more than ever, I see the need for the Samaritans. One of our basic needs is to be loved. It is a basic human need of every child, and all of us, to be seen and to be listened to . . .

> We have people from fifteen years of age up and I have met lots of young people in school who are actually in depression. At fourteen and fifteen they've almost lost hope and heart that there's anything worthwhile to live for. I've spoken to two parents in the last week whose children have threatened to do away with themselves, to commit suicide.

A survey into teenage depression was conducted in four Dublin schools during May, 1994. The students interviewed ranged in age from eleven to fifteen and the researchers found that depression is much more common among teenagers than is generally realised. Girls exhibit more symptoms than boys and about seventeen out of sixty-seven girls, in an all-girls school, and eight out of sixteen girls, in two special schools, showed some signs of depression. Four boys out of ninety-eight, in an all-boys school, also exhibited symptoms. All of the schools were in a "disadvantaged" area, an area in which depression would probably be double that of a middle-class area. The survey was conducted by Dr. Catherine McDonough, registrar in psychiatry at St. Vincent's Hospital, Fairview, and Dr. Michael Fitzgerald, a child psychiatrist in Dublin. They issued a questionnaire asking simple questions such as:

> Have you anyone to talk to?

> Do you get on with your family?

> Do you sometimes think life isn't worth living?

The authors of the questionnaire used it as a "pointer" of depression, one in which students could "score" in the depressive range. Such results would probably be much higher than the true total but would still be a good indicator of the number of students who might be clinically depressed or in need of treatment.

A number of factors such as family stress, medical problems, bullying or difficulties in keeping up at school may induce depression. Troublesome or particularly quiet children are often at risk and the source of the depression has to be identified before it can be dealt with. This can often result in the treatment of a parent's depression in order to treat that of the child.

Suicides are often concealed, under-reported or misrepresented by relatives, friends and police, a fact that hinders the effectiveness of any analytical study. Coroners describe the technicalities that have resulted in death, usually without stating that the victim died by his or her own hand. In 1860 the British started collecting statistics on suicide but these figures fluctuate, just like the crime rate, and are only of limited value when it comes to the study of suicide. Not all suicides can be proven as such, particularly in relation to drownings, car crashes or drug overdoses, so coroners often settle for a verdict of "death by misadventure".

Different people have different reasons for taking their own lives. Cecilia McEvoy's body was found in an open area called The Heath, outside Portlaoise, on 6 November, 1962. Nobody was ever arrested for her murder as the chief suspect drowned himself before he was charged. Detective Superintendent Murphy had no doubts about the man's guilt as he had interviewed him the night before he died.

Dr. Niamh Nic Daeid, a statistician and forensic scientist, worked on a study of suicide in conjunction with the Department of Epidemiology at the Royal College of Surgeons in Ireland. She remarked on how the suicide rate for those in the 15 - 24 age group had increased by one hundred per cent between 1982 and 1992. She noted that sixty-three per cent of men who committed suicide were single, that forty-nine per cent of women who killed themselves were married, and that Ireland has now one of the highest suicide rates in Europe.

Married men are less likely to commit suicide but Dr. Nic Daeid's report shows an increase in the suicide-rate for the 25 - 34 age group. Her figures for the younger age group increased by eighty per cent in three years, a statistic that places Ireland on a par with Britain where adolescent suicide is now so prevalent that it is listed as the third most common cause of death for young people, after accidents and cancer. Adolescents are unable to cope with anger and frustration and lack the experience of adult-type freedom. When they find themselves contained and constrained in a claustrophobic atmosphere, often being emotionally neglected, their unaccepted love and affection gradually turn to despair and depression. Problems associated with parents, school, work or romance are factors revealed as causes of adolescent suicide but emotionally-charged festivals can also engender suicide attempts by parasuicides.

In 1993 Yorkshire Television produced a booklet and television programme, each with the same title, *Deathwish: Surviving Suicide*, that commented on a startling increase in suicides by young men. Both noted that the ratio of young male suicides to female stood at four to one when the programme was transmitted on 23 May 1993. The researchers noted that the occupations of those likeliest to commit suicide were doctors, unskilled workers, veterinary surgeons, pharmacists, dentists, farmers, young men and male prisoners.

In the late 1960s and early 1970s several remand prisoners in Mountjoy made suicide attempts in order "to work their tickets" into the Central Mental Hospital in Dundrum. As many of those who attempted suicide were almost automatically transferred to this latter establishment they were able to benefit from its more relaxed atmosphere. As psychiatric patients, even convicted prisoners could avail of facilities such as wearing their own clothes, having their own individual cells and be in receipt of their own food and tobacco supplies. Visitors could also visit Dundrum more frequently than either the "Joy" (Mountjoy) or the "Bog" (Portlaoise) and were not restricted to monthly-only visits as they would have been in the other penal establishments.

The emerging drug culture of the 1970s and the AIDS-related diseases of the 1980s may have contributed to the changing pattern of prison life. A Kilkenny man claimed in 1970 that he was the "most-hanged" man in Ireland. He had pretended to hang himself from the bars of his cell-widow as the prison officer was passing his cell only to discover

111

that the prison officer passed by without looking through the Judas, a glassed-in peephole in the cell door. He released himself from his makeshift rope and waited for the officer's return only to be disappointed once again. He struggled in and out of that noose eleven times before his "attempted suicide" was discovered.

Twenty-three prisoners had killed themselves in Irish prisons over a sixteen-year-period by the time Fergal Bowers wrote his *Suicide in Ireland* (1994). Seventeen of them had hanged themselves from the cell-window bars. Sharon Gregg, a nineteen-year-old girl, serving a twelve-month sentence in Mountjoy, became the first woman prisoner to kill herself in living memory. Her last poem may shed some light on how she felt:

> I don't want to become bitter
>
> And filled with hate.
>
> I've seen too much hate
>
> I don't want to be angry anymore
>
> Forgive me please for what I have done
>
> And help me to live right again.

1994 was a particularly busy year in the Republic's prisons. Three prisoners hanged or asphyxiated themselves. Hanged may sound somewhat brutal but asphyxiated is such a nice way of saying someone was slowly strangled to death. The same Victorian cell-window bars are still serving a grim purpose for which they were never intended. Forty-two other prisoners, seven women and thirty-five men, attempted to kill themselves by hanging but were rescued before they were asphyxiated. The window bars are located about eight feet above floor level so prisoners are unable to achieve a sufficiently long drop to cause their own instantaneous deaths.

Eighteen prisoners tried to kill or injure themselves by swallowing various substances such as ground glass, razor blades or poisons and seven men set themselves on fire in their cells. One man died of a drugs overdose, a death that could be classified as suicide by stealth. A total of 216 prisoners required medical attention as a result of self-inflicted injuries, especially cuts to the throat, wrists, arms and legs. Razors and blades were used by thirteen females and one-hundred-and-seven males who inflicted various injuries on themselves.

Jim Cusack, writing in *The Irish Times* on Saturday, 6 May, 1995, stated that twenty-nine prisoners had committed suicide over the past ten years. Ten prisoners received medical treatment after they had overdosed on drugs and about half of the male, and most of the female, prisoners in Mountjoy are heroin addicts. A high level of the addicted prisoners are also HIV-positive.

A person may be committed to the Central Mental Hospital in Dundrum if he or she has been found "unfit to plead" during a court appearance on a criminal charge. Someone who has appeared in court to face charges but has established the defence of insanity may also be committed. Other people can be committed to the above institution by a process of civil commitment or "by an administrative act of the Minister for Justice transferring an inmate from his place of detention when he is found to be of unsound mind". Remand prisoners can also be transferred to the Central Mental Hospital if two surgeons or physicians certify that he or she is insane. At the time of writing Brendan O'Donnell charged with the murder of Imelda Riney and her son is the hospital's most recent patient and made a suicide attempt by trying to strangle himself.

Dr. Niamh Nic Daeid listed her high risk categories amongst the male suicides of Ireland, as farmers, unemployed men, the retired and skilled manual workers such as electricians carpenters and plumbers. The ratio of men and women who commit suicide in the six Ulster counties known as Northern Ireland was almost equal in the 1980s. This was at variance with the ratios elsewhere; five men to one woman in Poland; four men to one woman in Finland and Iceland; and two men to one woman in England and Wales by 1983, an increase in ratio from 1974 when the gap had narrowed to three men to two women.

The American experience of suicide seems to correspond with the Irish and British experiences in many respects. In 1988 Robert L. Crooks and Jean Stein noted how the incidence of suicide seemed to increase from adolescence onward, reaching a peak with the forty-five-year-old and older age groups. It was the tenth leading cause of death amongst American adults seeming to accelerate in May and October of each year, and was on the increase amongst adolescents and young adults, especially college students. Young people who are either homosexual or unsure of their sexual orientation may also be suicidal.

People have as many reasons for killing themselves as psychiatrists, doctors, psychologists, social workers and clergy have theories to propound. AIDS, alcoholism, ageing, blindness, broken homes,cancer, divorce, depression, drug addiction, epilepsy, family rows, gambling and homosexuality are but a few of the subjects blamed as the motivations behind acts of suicide. "The reasons given by the victims are understandable enough", wrote Prof. Erwin Stengel, "but they are hardly ever of a nature which would make suicide the only possible action to take". Unfortunately it is often impossible to determine why people commit suicide as the victims themselves are the only ones who could provide the relevant information.

Anger may provoke some people into taking their own lives. Hopelessness may be a key factor in many suicidal acts as it is the overall effect of problems, rather than the problems themselves, that may drive people to kill themselves. Mood disorders, post-natal depression, pressure at work, unemployment, financial worries and relationship difficulties may easily be contributing factors. Bereavement is another that should be taken into account and it may be induced by aspects other than death. The amputation of a limb, menopause, retirement, redundancy, or the loss of an ability, function or status can be just as devastating as death.

A young Vietnamese-born man hanged himself in St. Anne's Park, Raheny, in all probability a victim of persecution by gangs of youths who had tormented him with racial taunts. He was only eighteen-years-old, could not speak English very well and did not have a sense of belonging to either Ireland or Vietnam. Alan O'Keeffe interviewed the

114

young man's twenty-seven-year-old sister in the Sunday Independent of 30 April, 1995. She spoke of their childhood:

> I looked after him as a young child. We came through the war in Vietnam and through the seas on the boat. If we lost him then I might be able to understand it better . . . But not now, not in Ireland . . . his death really hurts.

Racism is usually directed at the travelling community but the Jewish, Chinese, Vietnamese and Indian communities have all suffered at one stage or another. The Jews of Limerick had to endure a two-year economic boycott from 1904 to 1906. This was engineered by Fr. John Creagh, a religious bigot, who wanted to start a credit union in the city. He was afraid to target the influential Protestant and Catholic merchants who would have made life intolerable for him so he attacked the trading practices of the tiny Jewish minority in Collooney Street (now Wolfe Tone Street). Their trading practices were no different than those of their Christian neighbours. This sorry episode resulted in most of the Jews being driven out of the city and became known as the "Limerick Pogrom".

The suicide rate of Asian women in the United Kingdom, in the sixteen to twenty-four-year-old age group, rose to three times that of the native British women between 1982 and 1992. Young Asian men, however, are more resilient than their native British peers, a reversal of the trend amongst the sexes. Family conflict, cultural pressures, conservative parental values and growing racism have been blamed for this trend in suicidal behaviour. Self-burning, or suttee, is the most favoured system or self-killing amongst Asian women. This is a particularly violent, painful and gruesome way in which to die. In 1991 fifty-one cases of suicide by burning were examined in England and Wales. Thirty-four of the forty-one male victims, and seven of the ten female ones, were white. This method of suicide is not common in Britain or Ireland although there is a well-documented record of one such "immolation" in a Limerick City bar on 27 September, 1995. People with schizophrenia and Asian-born women were over-represented in the British study of 1991.

Suicide attempts by young black women increased dramatically in the late 1970s and many young blacks and Asians are now growing up in a British society where they can be subject to racist attacks or discrimination. Unfortunately the Irish often imitate British trends and there appears to be a definite racist undercurrent in Irish society.

Arthur Griffith, Seán South of Garryowen and Oliver J. Flannagan were well known for their racist remarks at a time when it was almost a crime to be a liberal or a communist. People were discriminated against because of their religious and political views into the 1960s. Ireland could safely say it had no colour problem into modern times but then, again, it had little racial diversity except for a handful of foreign students, some medical and nursing staff, an occasional nun, priest, or professional and the rare casual worker. The influx of Asians in the 1970s and 1980s is very much a phenomenon of today.

Alcohol has a depressing effect, reducing inhibitions and self-control. It releases aggressive homicidal and suicidal impulses, and is often consumed by people before they attempt or commit suicide. In some instances an overindulgence in alcohol could almost be described as suicide by stealth. Many notable literary figures persisted in imbibing alcohol even though they knew their drinking was out of control. John Ryan wrote of the late Brendan Behan (1923-1964) and of how his drinking:

> . . . which was entirely self-inspired and self-motivated, had taken on epic proportions. He had passed from drinkard to drunkard to alcoholic and, finally, to dipsomaniac.

Brendan Behan suffered from diabetes and any consumption of alcohol would have upset his body's ability to produce its own glucose. He persisted in drinking even though he knew, as a diabetic, that he should avoid alcohol. His excessive thirst, however, may easily have been a symptom of poorly controlled diabetes, an irritating ache that could be temporarily relieved by intakes of fluid.

The largest mass suicide of modern times occurred on 18 November 1978. Jim Jones, the leader of the People's Temple Cult, and 910 of his

116

followers killed themselves, by taking cyanide, in Guyana.

During the Christmas season of 1977, John Helmes, an artist who was unable to face the future, made the most spectacular unsuccessful suicide attempt to date. He jumped off the eighty-sixth floor of the Empire State Building in New York but was blown onto a ledge on the eighty-fifth floor by a gust of wind which he interpreted as a sign of divine intervention. He knocked on an office window and was admitted by the staff.

Animals may die as a result of their actions but only man commits suicide. Glanville Williams wrote of animal suicide as a manifestation of intelligence in the Quarterly Journal of Criminal Psychopathology in 1943. He mentioned dogs committing suicide by drowning or refusing food for a variety of reasons, including abandonment, boredom, desertion, regret and remorse. In 1985 Jacqueline N. Crawley wrote of how "stress-causing situations such as crowding, isolation, separation and confinement, especially when uncontrollable, can result in self-destructive and self-endangering behaviour" in captive and domesticated animals.

In 1963 Louis Dublin wrote of how the American insurance companies found in favour of 'death from natural causes' when suicide occurred as a result of mental disorder. If a policy holder committed suicide within two years of taking out insurance they had protected themselves by insisting on a clause which provided for the return of the premium, without interest. The two-year clause did not apply where suicide was considered as a symptom of illness and suicide has not posed a problem to Irish, British or American insurance companies in the succeeding years. The same maxim still applies to a certain extent. The Irish Progressive Assurance Company, now part of the Irish Permanent Group, will pay out on a policy if the death takes place one year and a day from the inception date of the policy. This course is based on the original proposal form having been completed truthfully.

There are many documented and undocumented aspects of suicide of which we know very little. It may be possible to commit suicide by stealth if one is a diabetic, coeliac or suffering from a food allergy of some kind. One only has to eat the wrong foods in order to kill oneself in a manner few coroners would care to return a verdict on. Alcoholics and drug addicts may also fit into categories of those who commit suicide by stealth insofar as their lifestyles may terminate their lives long before they would have died of natural causes. Suicide is often presaged by a statement of intent as anyone who intends killing himself or herself will most likely tell somebody else about their proposal to do so. This period will be followed by a subtle change in the suicidal person's demeanour and oblique hints will testify to the victim's intentions. "I guess I won't be seeing you again", may be the gist of throwaway remarks or someone might say "good-bye", instead of "good day" or "good night". Making a will, tidying up affairs and giving away possessions are further clues of the victim's proposed intention. This will be followed by a calm and tranquil period as the suicidal person comes to terms with his or her decision.

The changing pattern of modern life in an industrialised society has broken up the more traditional agricultural family structure. In the past every member of the family had a different role. The older generation, the grandparents, looked after their grandchildren, the younger generation worked on the land, and children were regarded as social and economic assets who could assist their parents and grandparents from an early age. Modern housing is designed with young couples in mind, has barely enough room for parents and their children, and has little or no space for grandparents who are either left to fend for themselves or enter a nursing-home for the elderly or infirm. This renders old people very vulnerable. It lowers their self-esteem, making them feel unwanted, rejected and useless, with little or no future, and often drives them to suicide out of sheer loneliness.

The incidence of suicide keeps pace with age, the risk increasing progressively as people grow older, with the highest rates of suicide being found amongst sixty-five-year-olds.

Suicidal people seem to have several common characteristics. One can start to think of suicide as he or she seeks a solution to a specific problem. He or she can visualise death as a means of relieving or escaping some awful psychological pain and as a method of dealing with some frustrated psychological need or thwarted desire. A feeling of intense helplessness or hopelessness can leave the suicidal person in a state where he or she feels unable to solve problems. The suicidal person will also endure a period of indecision as he or she has ambivalent feelings, wonders about whether or not to go ahead with the decision to commit suicide or simply make an attempt that could be construed as a cry for help.

The option of killing oneself or staying alive is debated or examined by the suicidal person who sees everything on a black or white basis. He or she will use extremes of language featuring words like "always" and "never" and take an "all or nothing" view of his or her existence. Regression is another characteristic of the suicidal person who will dwell on his or her past in much the same way as a child might run away from home. An open, oblique or hidden notification of the person's intention of committing suicide will be given at some stage, occasionally in the form of a suicide note. The prospective suicide is usually a perfectionist in some aspect of life, cannot tolerate uncertainty and has coping patterns that are impaired when it comes to problem solving.

Feelings of uselessness in the elderly who are unable to accept retirement may lead to thoughts of suicide. They are often lonely, isolated or widowed. They may suffer from chronic physical disabilities such as deafness or bronchitis and may believe that they are no longer wanted by their families, friends or communities.

Leaving Certificate results caused the Association of Secondary Teachers, Ireland (ASTI) to remark on how the issuing of results, on Thursday, 18 August, 1994 was a high-risk time for attempted suicides. The association also warned parents to be alert as the examination points system and competition for university places put their children under pressure to succeed. Seán Higgins, the president of the ASTI, asked parents to be extra sympathetic, to avoid discussions in relation to high expectations and not to betray "their own outspoken but sometimes inflated expectations".

The children of alcoholic families often believe themselves to be the source of all the problems encountered by the family. They suffer from low self-esteem, guilt, remorse and frustration at not realising alcoholism is a disease, and often isolate themselves by denying anything is happening because they find alcoholism impossible to deal with. David Stafford, author of *Children of Alcoholics* (1994), states that there are three basic rules in an alcoholic family. The first means that one does not talk about problems, particularly drinking; the second rule stipulates that one should be devoid of feeling about the problem, thus denying that it exists; and the third notes the problem children have in developing trust with a parent who breaks promises, has a fit of remorse and yet makes the innocent party feel guilty because he or she felt angry at the parent's lapse. Such children may become depressed because of extreme anger, rage and feelings of loss,loss of childhood, loss of home environment, loss of parents and loss of self or self-esteem.

Thirty per cent of youth suicides are amongst gay adolescents, according to Cathal Kelly in an article in *The Irish Times* of Monday, 24 April, 1995. He wrote of the alarming suicide rate among young gays, stating that it was the leading cause of death amongst this peer group. He also mentioned how thirty to fifty per cent of gay teenagers attempted suicide stating that almost half of those lesbian and gay young people who do attempt suicide make repeated attempts, and noted how gay adolescents are two to three times more likely to attempt suicide than their heterosexual peers.

Twenty-three TDs and Senators spoke in the 1993 debates on the decriminalisation of suicide but only one, Senator David Norris, spoke of the higher rate of suicide among young gay people. The 1994 Report of the Expert Advisory Group on Relationship and Sexuality Education advocated that sex education should be delivered in a school environment. It cited young people's dissatisfaction with their preparation in school for forming relationships with friends of the opposite sex and only mentioned sexual orientation towards the end.

Young homosexuals are prone to suicide or suicidal thoughts from an early stage. Their problems can start in school when they are taunted, insulted, bullied, humiliated or beaten by their schoolmates. As they grow older, their tormentors' capacity for cruelty seems to increase and young homosexuals can become quite isolated and depressed by the time they are ready to leave school. Cathal Kelly and P.A. McLaughlin became aware of this suicidal tendency when they worked on helplines and amongst the gay community. McLaughlin abandoned the helpline because he became too emotionally involved in his callers' problems. He is still an active gay campaigner and researcher with a Northern Ireland group. Cathal Kelly worked on a Limerick helpline which was established after two homosexuals killed themselves in Limerick. He is now editor of the Gay Community News and believes that suicide will remain a problem as long as homosexuality is "officially sidelined" in Ireland.

Kate Hill died of a brain haemorrhage in July, 1994, at the age of twenty-nine. Her book *The Long Sleep - Young People and Suicide*, was published, posthumously, in May, 1995. She was a brilliant research worker and confined her study to the examination of suicidal behaviour amongst the young people of today. She wrote of how suicide is the leading cause of death among gay, lesbian and bisexual youth in the United States. Kate Hill recorded how suicide attempts were more common among the young homosexual community than amongst their heterosexual peers and stated that homosexual males were six times more likely, and lesbians twice as likely, to attempt suicide as their heterosexual counterparts. Most of these suicide attempts were made by people under the age of twenty-one.

AIDS is a modern acronym derived from the initials for Acquired Immune Deficiency Syndrome. This simple four-letter acronym refers to an often fatal group of concurrent symptoms of a disease, probably the most dreaded disease in today's world. It can infect people at any stage, usually with fatal results, and those infected, their families and friends can become quite suicidal. AIDS became known as "the gay plague" in the United States. It was particularly prevalent among the homosexual and drug-addicted communities but is now on the increase, worldwide, amongst heterosexuals and homosexuals alike. Dr. James Walsh was the government's special adviser on AIDS until January, 1995. He told Maeve Sheehan of *The Sunday Tribune*, in an interview published on 19 February, 1995, that he expected a "third wave" of the AIDS epidemic to hit Ireland over the next ten years. He believes AIDS is no longer "in the public mind" as there has been an increase in sexually transmitted diseases, a statistic which means that people are indulging in unprotected sex. He referred to how the future of HIV and AIDS depended on the degree in which it spread within the heterosexual population and that AIDS could already be described as a plague.

Pat Tierney was a poet, author, wanderer, street entertainer, AIDS activist and AIDS sufferer. He met Brenda Power, a journalist with The Sunday Tribune, on Tuesday and Wednesday, 2 and 3 January, 1996, and told her that he intended to kill himself on Thursday 4 January, the day of his thirty-ninth birthday. He was born in Galway, the son of an unmarried seventeen-year-old woman and was raised in a series of charitable Catholic institutions suffering sexual, physical and emotional abuse. He contacted AIDS in Arizona from a contaminated needle soon after he had emigrated there. He had got in touch with the newspaper in order to discuss his inpending suicide because he wanted his many friends to know that he was neither insane nor in despair:

> I'm doing this because I feel spent, finished, and it's time for me to go on. I see is as a positive thing, of taking control of my life and my death, and people who know me, though they will be grieving, should try to see it like that. I don't want to go on climbing mountains, I don't want to fight anymore. Basically, I'm throwing in the towel. And the beauty of my suicide is that I don't allow the church, the state or any supposedly-existing deity to decide when I quench the light.

In 1993 Pat Tierney published his autobiography, *The Moon on my Back*, the story of a lifetime of misery, loneliness, abuse and rejection. His body was found, hanging from a tree, in the grounds of Corpus Christi Church, Griffith Avenue, Dublin, on Friday, 5 January, 1996.

Asking a friend or relative if they are suicidal is a question from which many people shy away. Posing such questions will not increase the risk of someone committing suicide and may actually be the first step in helping someone through a crisis. In 1990 an American doctor, Eric Berne, noted that death, by suicide or homicide, was no solution to life's problems and suggested that anyone contemplating either should pay attention to his "two inviolable rules". Rule number one stated that no parent should be allowed to die until all of his or her children were over eighteen. Rule number two said that no child should commit suicide while either of his or her parents were still alive. People contemplating suicide, however, regularly violate these rules as they are already committed to a course of action regardless of Eric Berne's, or anyone else's, advice.

A comforting religious faith or philosophy of life can be a crucial factor in determining whether or not someone will die by his or her own hand. Erwin Stengel wrote of how the decline of religious beliefs and the laxity of professional and marital behaviour had disturbed the social fabric reducing people's immunity against suicidal tendencies. He explained the high incidence of suicide amongst the divorced and other people who were without supportive networks.

On 3 December, 1995 John Dunne of the National Youth Federation estimated that suicide was the single biggest killer of young men aged between eighteen and thirty-four years of age. Research by his organisation blamed the increase in suicide on the decline of the traditional family, the slump in the influence of the various churches and "the growing polarisation of young people between those who were performing brilliantly from an academic point of view and those who were not." The academic prowess of young women may also have some significant bearing on the fact that fewer young women kill themselves than young men.

Suicides are a cause of pain, guilt and anger. They can split families as various members try to come to terms with their grief. The bereaved find it extremely hard to express anger against themselves, the suicide victim, the community and their God. Friends and family members can be made scapegoats as recrimination are cast and people try to blame the living in order to shed their own feelings of guilt. The bereaved can be the prey of very mixed emotions as they experience the reality of loss. They have to adjust to a changed environment and may withdraw emotional energy to re-invest in other relationships, only to feel that they may be "betraying" the suicide victim.

A family history of suicide may be described as a collective refusal to survive, according to Erwin Stengel in his *Suicide & Attempted Suicide* (1964). He found no evidence to support the theory of some families having an innate predisposition to suicide and believed that there were specific or special reasons why one member of a family should emulate the suicide of another. He dismissed the idea of one member of the family imitating another in such circumstances unless his or her mind was tending in that direction.

The bereaved are the forgotten victims of suicide. Psychiatrist Dr. Moosajee Bhamjee allowed me to look through his unpublished notes, *"The Suicide Bereaved"*:

> The gardaí, clergy, doctor and support groups will be of assistance to the bereaved but it is essential to know how to assist the bereaved who are in a state of shock, numb with pain and asking themselves multiple questions of "why" and "if" as they agonise over their feelings.

> The family is affected by a feeling of failure, guilt, rejection, frustration and hopelessness, with an occasional twinge of anger because th deceased did not seek help from the family. The parents can feel cheated because all their hopes, ambitions and plans for a dead child's future are destroyed and fears for their other children develop. A spouse will feel that he or she was not trusted by the dead partner and the children should be gently informed and allowed to participate in funeral arrangements.

> Grandparents are also affected by a grandchild's suicide. Each family and every individual member will need to adjust to the loss but the carer and community must be available to listen and offer help and time. The unanswerable question of "why" will constantly be asked and the carer must help with acceptance of the death and assist family or others to reconstruct their lives. An explanation of

grief might help as the bereaved can feel stressed. It might be necessary after a time to have either tranquillisers or antidepressants prescribed for the bereaved, for a short period, because they may not eat or sleep and may neglect themselves. They could also be referred to self- help bereavement groups or be befriended by the Samaritans.

Supporting young suicide bereaved must be addressed as their reactions and needs are different and some timely help might prevent 'copycat' suicides occurring. The youngsters need to attend the funeral and be "chief- mourners" if necessary. The school should arrange a memorial service and a teacher, parents or counsellor should be available to discuss the youngsters' concerns. A group discussion can help and allowing the children to express their views and feelings will be beneficial.

It is important to deglorify the suicide and to discourage any rumours. It is also important to keep an eye on people who become lonely and isolate themselves and those who talk of death. Sometimes the family doctor, clergyman or carer will need to discuss his or her feelings too for he or she may have known the deceased for years and will suffer the after-effects as much as the rest of the family, friends or community.

Leslie Marron, of the Monaghan-based Bereavement Society, was interviewed by Brenda Power in *The Sunday Tribune* of 30 April, 1995. He spoke of how his group encountered an unexpected response to the first meeting which was devoted entirely to those bereaved by suicide. He expected eight or nine people to attend but was astonished when thirty relatives showed up. Brenda Power wrote:

Struck by the number of young men among those who had taken their own lives, Mr. Marron spoke informally to some of the affected families in a bid to find some common denominator. "A lot of them were in good jobs, had girlfriends, seemed to have everything going for them", he says. "One angle I was following up was that a large number of them appeared to have been to a disco that night or the night before - it could be that the bright lights and the loud music give some kind of a false high". Other research seems to back up the notion that some of these young men may have found themselves in an incongruously jolly social situation shortly before their deaths - a recent study in one Irish county found that 14 young male suicides had all taken a small amount of alcohol just before they kill themselves.

The subject of death is a taboo subject in the modern world. Euphemisms such as "passed away" are used to soften the impact and suicide is virtually unmentionable. The stigma attached to suicide has lessened in recent times but it is a subject that seems to have been virtually ignored in modern urban folklore.

AFTERWORD

I can offer no solutions but this afterword is a reminder of those volunteers who are always at the end of the line, the Samaritans. They exist to help the suicidal, lonely or despairing. They do this by listening without offering advice, criticism or judgement, have an apolitical non-sectarian approach and pride themselves on being non-judgmental. They provide a sympathetic and confidential support for people who feel life is no longer worth living and can empathise with those thoughts and feelings people are unable, or ashamed, to discuss with family or friends.

The Samaritans always ask people if they are feeling suicidal and find that most people interpret the question as part of a caring inquiry, one to which they can respond. The Samaritans use this question as a psychological "ice-breaker" and utilise it to help people through crisis situations. They allow people the ultimate freedom of choice, to live or die by their own reckoning. In 1964 Erwin Stengel noted that one quarter of the Samaritan membership was comprised of people who were former clients although I believe the organisation uses the term callers rather than clients today. A lot of people who are good in supportive roles tend to get depressed, a fact that places Samaritan volunteers in a high-risk category. Anybody can be suicidal, and being suicidal is not necessarily a bar to being a Samaritan volunteer. It would be a bar if the person was suicidal at the time of joining or shortly before doing so.

Suicide has always inspired fear and been treated as a taboo subject but nowadays many young people, and some older ones, have an almost pathological inability to come to terms with any form of death, accidental, natural or suicidal.

More than half of female suicides are committed by housewives, according to an article in the *Evening Press* on Thursday, 10 November. Chris Macey was quoting a Samaritan spokeswoman, Alice Conroy, who said that improved methods of reporting suicides were partly responsible for the higher figure of self-inflicted deaths in the twenty-five to thirty-four age group. There was a genuine increase in the amount of people wishing to take their own lives and young farmers were identified as the people most at risk.

Dr. Moosajee Bhamjee's reflections on suicide are probably the most fitting words on which to close this book. I listened to him on Saturday, 10 February, 1996 and took notes on what he had to say on the subject:

> The tide of suicide continues to rise. It is a wave that is sweeping the nation. Will the wave ever flatten as the numbers in the sixteen to thirty-five-year-old age group rise? And the under-twelves are now committing suicide, four in 1994 alone. The Irish population has two extremes, the youth and the elderly, and the rate of suicide in both groups is high. No more is it a male prerogative as women are catching up with men and the rural rate of suicide is rising to equal the urban rate
>
> As we move from a rural economy to an urban one, come to terms with new managerial styles and confront the prevailing "market force" society and the new ideas pertaining to the same, will our approach to suicide change? Will our acceptance of suicide be a factor to encourage suicide?
>
> Will the increased rates of depression in our society result in an increase in the level of prescribed antidepressants? Will society bind itself once more to protect the "vulnerable stock"? Time will tell.

The Samaritan telephone lines are manned day and night, twenty-four hours a day, north and south of the border. People can also contact them by letter or call in person to any of their eighteen centres scattered around Ireland, ten in the Republic and eight in Northern Ireland.

1850 - 60 - 90 - 90 is a single low-cost telephone number for the Samaritans that came into operation in the Republic, in September 1993. This enables suicidal callers to ring the Samaritans from any private telephone, anywhere in the twenty-six southern counties, for any length of time, at the cost of a local call. Specific branches can also be contacted by dialling the following numbers, calling to the listed addresses between 10.00a.m and 10.00p.m. or by writing to the Samaritans:

3 Court Devenish Athlone 0902 - 73133

Coach Street Cork 021 - 271323

112 Marlborough Street Dublin 01 - 8727700

"Sunville", Kilrush Road Ennis 065 - 29777

14 Nuns' Island Galway 091 - 561222 20 Barrington Street Limerick 061 - 412111

3 McIlwaine Terrace Newbridge 045 - 435299

12 Chapel Street Sligo 071 - 42011

44 Moyderwell Tralee 066 - 22566

16 Beau Street Waterford 051 - 72114

0345 - 90 - 90 - 90 is a single low-cost telephone number that the Samaritans in Britain share with some of their colleagues on the Irish mainland, linking the United Kingdom with the eight centres in Northern Ireland:

45 Mount Street Ballymena 01266 - 650000

92 Dufferin Avenue, Bangor Bangor &

North Down 01247 - 464646

5 Wellesley Avenue Belfast 01232 - 664422

20 Lodge Road Coleraine 01265 - 320000

162 Thomas Street,

Portadown Craigavon 01762 - 333555

16 Clarendon Street Derry 01504 - 265511

19 St. Colman's Park Newry 01693 - 66366 20 Campsie Road Omagh 01662 - 244944

Acknowledgments

Suicide is a particularly awkward subject to research but it is no longer ignored in the modern world. I delved into Irish history, myth and folklore to find examples of famous people who had killed themselves and was able to unearth the relevant information from the works of, amongst others: David Beresford, Henry Boylan, Anne M.Brady, Moyra Caldecott, Nora Chadwick, Liam Clarke, Brian Cleeve, Davis Coakley, Tim Pat Coogan, Seán Cronin, Kevin Danaher, Frank Delaney, Patrick S. Dinneen, J.E. Doherty, Michael V. Duignan, Peter Berresford Ellis, John Fleetwood, R.F. Foster, Peter Harbison, D.J. Hickey, Reg Hindley, Hans Holzer, Henri Hubert, P.W. Joyce, Fergus Kelly, Lord Killanin, Dorothy Macardle, Frank MacDermot, Uninseann MacEoin, Edward MacLysaght, Maire Mac Neill, Nell McCafferty, F.X. Martin, T.W. Moody, Des Moore, Seamus O Cathain, Brian O'Cuiv, Padraic O'Farrell, Daithi O' hOgain, Mairtin O Murchu, Seán O'Suilleabhain, Rosemary Cullen Owens, T.G.E.Powell, Patrick C. Power, Joseph Raftery, Anne Ross Peter Somerville-Large and Edward Walford. I learned more about suicide and its effects from the books of A. Alvarez, Raymond Byrne, Mavis Arnold, Susan Bassnett, Fergal Bowers, Hugh Brody, Cathal B. Daly, Paddy Doyle, Emile Durkheim, Gerard Green, R. Leighton Hasselrodt, Kate Hill, Gerard W. Hogan, J.B. Keane, Heather Laskey, Derek Llewellyn-Jones, Paul McDermot, Sylvia Plath, Terry Prone, David Reuben, Nickie Roberts, Ailbhe Symth and Erwin Stengel. The bibliography contains more complete details of the books consulted as well as a listing of articles from various newspapers and journals by Liz Allen, Joseph Baker, Dr. Moosajee Bhamjee, Ann Cahill, Geraldine Collins, Jim Cusack, Martin Cowley, Jacqueline N. Crawley, Penelope Dening,Willie Dillon, Stephen Dodd, Trish Hegarty, Kathryn Holmquist, Ann Holohan, Kenneth Kearon, M.J. Kelleher, Andrew Kelly, Cathal Kelly, Geraldine Kennedy, Susan McKay, Michael MacUileagoid, Robert Matthews, Kevin Moore, Yvonne Moran, Dave Mullins, Mary Mulvihill, Imogen O'Connor, Nuala O Faolain, Nollaig O Gadhra, Alan O'Keeffe, Eileen O' Leary, Peter Pallot, Andy Pollak, Brenda Power, David Prosser, Arthur Quinlan, Maeve Sheehan, Kathy Sheridan, Frank Symth and Gillian Tindall. I would also like to pay a special tribute to the outstanding work of two women in the field of suicide research, Niamh NicDaeid, in Ireland, and the late Kate Hill, in Britain.

This book is, in part, a compilation of their works augmented by material gleaned from many other people. Some contributors preferred to remain anonymous but supplied information that I would not have found otherwise.

I would like to take this opportunity to express my gratitude to those just mentioned and to all of the following:

Michael Beatty, Galway.

Claire Bhamjee, Ennis

Dr. Moosajee Bhamjee, T.D., Ennis.

Helen Billinghurst, London.

Deirdre Casey, Ennis.

Mary Cashin, Ennis.

Maureen Comber, Ennis.

Willie Conneely, Galway.

Siobhan Considine, Ennis.

Dr. Frank Counihan, Ennis.

Gerry Dore, Limerick.

Dervilla Evans, Ennis.

Maeve S. Fitzgibbon, Ennis.

Pat Flynn, Ennis.

Eddie Frost, Limerick.

Seamus Garry, Cootehill.

Mary Garry, London.

Michael Gibbons, Clifden.

Sigie Gilger, Kilmaley.

Rev. Bob Hanna, Ennis.

Joe Hayes, Limerick.

Michael Hegarty, Clarecastle.

Padraig Hegarty, Claremorris.

Susanne Heringklee, Galway.

Jim Higgins, Galway.

Rev. Joe Hourigan, Ennis.

Seán Killeen, Miltown Malbay.

Harry Hughes, Miltown Malbay.

Annette Kennelly, Ennis.

Edmund Lenihan, Crusheen.

Desmond Long, Corbally, Limerick.

Dr. Patricia Lynch, Limerick.

Seán McCarthy, Ennis.

Ger Madden, Whitegate.

Joseph Mangan, Ennis.

Michael Meaney, Lissycasey.

Joe Meehan, Castletroy, Limerick.

Kevin Merry, Dorchester, U.S.A.

Frank Moore, Ennis.

Tony Moore, Ennis.

John Mulkerrins, Ennis.

Tom Munnelly, Miltown Malbay.

Paddy Naughton, Ennis.

Michael Nihill, Ennis.

Dr. Aine Ni Riain, Ennis.

Michelle O' Brien, Ennis.

John O'Brien, Drumline.

Pat O'Brien, Clonlara

Jeff O'Connell, Kinvara.

Brian O Dalaigh, Castleknock, Dublin.

John O'Donnell, Galway.

John O'Dwyer, Newport, Tipperary.

Frances O'Gorman,, Ennis.

P. J. O'Halloran, Ennis.

Dr. Rory O'Keefe, Ennis.

Kevin O'Kelly, Galway.

Gerry O'Leary, Tralee.

Dr. Ciaran O Murchadha, Ennis.

Rose O'Sullivan, Ennis.

Tomas Ryan, Ennis.

Michelle Sayers, Ennis.

Sonia Schorman, Ballyalla, Ennis.

Mattie Shannon, Doolin.

Michael Shannon, Doolin.

Irene Spelliscy, Edmonton, Canada.

Sinead Spellissy, Ennis.

Isobel Stokes, Ennis.

Michael Stokes, Clonmel.

Ina Tagney, Ennis.

Neddy and Mary Talty, Old Kilcash.

Dr. Maurice Ward, Ennis.

BIBLIOGRAPHY OF SOURCE MATERIAL.

BOOKS

Allen, R.E., Editor, *The Concise Oxford Dictionary of Current English,* eighth edition, Oxford, 1990.

Alvarez, A., *Day of Atonement,* London, 1991.

Alvarez, A., *The Savage God. A Study of Suicide,* Middlesex, 1971.

Arnold, Mavis and Heather Laskey, *Children of the Poor Clares, The Story of an Irish Orphanage,* Belfast, 1985.

Arrowsmith, Nancy, with George Moose, *A Field Guide to the Little People,* London, 1977, 1978.

A Short Guide to Mental Illness for the Family Doctor, Dagenham, 1966.

Bassnett, Susan, *Women Writers. Sylvia Plath,* London, 1987.

Beresford, David, *Ten Dead Men. The Story of the 1981 Irish Hunger Strike,* London, 1987.

Berne, Eric, M.D., *What Do You say After You Say Hello? The Psychology of Human Destiny,* Beverly Hills, 1990 edition.

Bowers, Fergal, *Suicide in Ireland,* Dublin, 1994.

Boylan, Henry, *A Dictionary of Irish Biography,* second edition, Dublin.

Bowler, Peter, *What a Way to Go! Some of the Strangest Deaths on Record,* edited by Johnathan Green, London, 1983.

Brady, Anne M., and Brian Cleeve, *A Biographical Dictionary of Irish Writers,* Gigginstown, 1985.

Brody, Hugh, Inishkillane. *Change and Decline in the West of Ireland,* London, 1973.

Brown, J.A.C., *Pears Medical Encylopaedia,* London, 1962.

Bunreacht na hEireann (Constitution of Ireland), Diachtaigh an Pobal an 1 Iuil, 1937 (Enacted by the people Ist July, 1937) - I ngniomh on 29 Nollaig, 1937 (In operation as from 29th December, 1937).

Byrne, Raymond, Gerard W. Hogan and Paul McDermot *Prisoners' Rights. A Study in Irish Prison Law,* Dublin, 1981.

Caldecott, Moyra, *Women in Celtic Myth*, London, 1988.

Canon Law Society of Great Britain and Ireland, The, in association with The Canon Law Society of Australia and New Zealand and The Canadian Canon Law Society, The Code of Canon Law, London, Sydney Dublin, 1983, published with index, 1984.

Catechism of the Catholic Church, Dublin, 1994.

Chadwick, Nora, *The Celts*, Harmondsworth, 1979.

Clare Tourist Council, *A Guide to County Clare,* Treoran do Conndae an Clair, Limerick.

Clarke, Liam, *Broadening the Battlefield*. The H-Blocks and the Rise of Sinn Féin, Dublin, 1987.

Clements, Jonathan, *Crazy But True,* London, 1986.

Coakley, Davis, *The Irish School of Medicine. Outstanding Practitioners of the 19th Century,* Dublin, 1988.

Coogan, Tim Pat, *The I.R.A.,* Glasgow, 1988.

Cronin, Seán, *Irish Nationalism. A History of its Roots and Ideology,* Dublin, 1980.

Crooks, Robert L., and Jean Stein, *Psychology, Science, Behaviour and Life,* New York, 1988.

Daly, Cathal B., *Morals, Law and Life. An Examination of the book: The Sanctity of Life and the Criminal Law,* Dublin, London.

Danaher, Kevin, *Gentle Places and Simple Things,* Cork, 1964.

Danaher, Kevin, *Irish Country People,* Cork, 1982.

Danaher, Kevin, *The Year in Ireland. Irish Calendar Customs,* Dublin, Cork, Minnesota, 1972.

De Bhaldraithe, Tomas, *English-Irish Dictionary,* Baile Atha Cliath, 1959.

Delaney, Frank, *Legends of the Celts,* London, 1991.

De-la-Noy, Michael, *Acting as Friends. The Story of the Samaritans*, London, 1989.

De Rosa, Peter, Vicars of Christ. *The Dark Side of the Papacy,* London, 1988, 1989.

Diagram Group, *Man's Body. An Owner's Manual,* London, 1976.

Dinneen, Rev. Patrick S., *Focloir Gaedhilge agus Bearla, An Irish-English Dictionary,* Dublin, Cork, 1927.

Donleavy, J.P., *The Unexpurgated Code. A Complete Manual of Survival & Manners,* London, 1975.

Doolan, Brian, *Principles of Irish Law,* Dublin, 1981.

Doolan, Brian, *Principles of Irish Law,* (third edition), Dublin, 1992.

Doyle, Lynn, *An Ulster Childhood,* Belfast, 1921, 1985.

Doyle, Paddy, *The God Squad* - A Remarkable True Story, London, 1989.

Dublin Lesbian and Gay Men's Collectives, *Out for Ourselves, The Lives of Irish Lesbians and Gay Men,* Dublin, 1986.

Durkheim,Emile, Suicide. *A Study in Sociology,* translated by John A. Spaulding and George Simpson, from the 1930 edition, original edition 1897, Toronto, 1951, 1968.

Drury, M.I., K. Coonan, D. Creegan & M. Beggan, *Understanding Your Diabetes,* Dublin, 1984.

Ellis, Peter Berresford, *The Celtic Empire. The First Millennium of Celtic History 1,000BC - 51AD,* London, 1990.

Enno, Stephen, *Spies in Ireland*, London, 1963.

Fleetwood, John, *The Irish Body Snatchers. A History of Body Snatching in Ireland,* Dublin, 1988.

Foster, R.F., *Modern Ireland 1600-1972*, London, 1988.

Gleeson, John, *The Book of Irish Lists and Trivia,* Dublin, 1989.

Green, Gerard, *Coping with Suicide. A Pastoral Aid,* Blackrock, 1992.

Harbison, Peter, *Pre-Christian Ireland. From the First Settlers to the Early Celts,* London, 1988.

Hasselrodt, R. Leighton, *Twilight Women of the World. International Picture of the Other Love,* London, 1965.

Hayes, Richard J., Editor, *Sources for the History of Irish Civilisation.* Articles in Irish Periodicals, Boston, 1970.

Hickey, D.J., and J.E. Doherty, *A Dictionary of Irish History 1800-1980,* Dublin, 1989.

Hill, Kate, *The Long Sleep - Young People and Suicide,* London, 1995.

Hindley, Reg, *The Death of the Irish Language. A Qualified Obituary,* London, 1990.

Hinton, John, *Dying,* Harmondsworth, Middlesex, 1967, 1972.

Holzer, Hans, *The Lively Ghosts of Ireland,* New York, 1967.

Hubert, Henri, *The History of the Celtic People,* a one-volume edition, including, The Rise of the Celts and The Greatness and Decline of the Celts, London, 1993, originally published in 1934.

James, Philip S., *Introduction to English Law,* Tenth Edition, London, 1979.

Johnston, Edith Mary, *Ireland in the Eighteenth Century. The Gill History of Ireland,* Dublin, 1973.

Joyce, P.W., *A Smaller Social History of Ancient Ireland,* second edition, Dublin, 1908.

Keane, John B., *Letters of a Love-Hungry Farmer,* Dublin, Cork, 1974.

Kelly, Fergus, *A Guide to Early Irish Law,* Dublin, 1988, reprint 1991.

Killanin, Lord, & Michael V. Duignan, *The Shell Guide to Ireland,* London, 1967.

Kinzer, Nora Scott, *Stress and the American Woman,* New York, 1978, 1979.

Llewellyn-Jones, Derek, *Every Man,* Oxford University Press, 1982.

Lodge's Peerage, Baronetage, Knightage & Companionage of the British Empire for 1912, eighty-first edition, London, December 1911.

Lynam, Shevawn, *Humanity Dick Martin, 'King of Connemara', 1754-1834,* Dublin, 1989.

Lyons, F.S.L., *Ireland Since the Famine,* Suffolk, 1982.

Macardle, Dorothy, *The Irish Republic. A Documented Chronicle of the Anglo-Irish Conflict and the Partitioning of Ireland, with a Detailed Account of the period 1916-1923* with a Preface by Eamonn De Valera, London, 1968.

MacDermot, Frank, *Theobald Wolfe Tone and His Times,* Tralee, 1939, 1969.

MacDonald, A.M., Editor, *Chambers's Shorter English Dictionary,* London, 1955.

MacEoin, Uinseann, *Survivors.* New and Enlarged Edition, Dublin, 1987.

MacLysaght, Edward, *Irish Life in the Seventeenth Century,* Cork, 1939.

MacNeill, Maire, *The Festival of Lughnasa - a study of the survival of the celtic festival of the beginning of harvest,* Dublin, 1982.

McCafferty, Nell, *The Armagh Women,* Dublin, 1981.

Mitchell, Ross, *Depression,* Middlesex, 1983.

Moody, T.W., and F.X. Martin, *The Course of Irish History,* Cork, revised edition, 1983.

Moore, Des, *Off-beat Ireland,* Naas.

Nown, Graham, and Bill Tidy, *Bill Tidy's Book of Classic Cock-Ups,* Sevenoaks, Kent, 1985.

O Cathain, Seamas, *Irish Life and Lore,* Dublin, Cork, 1982.

O' Cuiv, Brian, Editor, *A View of the Irish Language,* Dublin, 1969.

O' Farrell, Padraic, *Superstitions of the Irish Country People,* Cork, Dublin, 1978, 1982.

O'Farrell, Padraic, *Who's Who in the Irish War of Independence 1916-1920,* Dublin, Cork, 1980.

Ogilvie, John, Editor, The Imperial Dictionary, English, Technological, and Scientific; adapted to the present state of literature, science and art; on the basis of Webster's English Dictionary, Glasgow, Edinburgh, London, 1850.

O hOgain, Dr. Daithi, Myth, Legend & Romance - *An Encyclopaedia of the Irish Folk Tradition,* New York, 1991.

O Luing, Seán, *I Die in a Good Cause. A Study of Thomas Ashe, idealist and revolutionary,* Tralee, 1970.

O Murchu, Mairtin, *The Irish Language,* Dublin, 1985.

O Riordain, Seán P., *Antiquities of the Irish Countryside,* New York, 1984 edition.

O Suileabhain, Seán, *Irish Wake Amusements, Cork, 1961,* 1967.

Owens, Rosemary Cullen, *Smashing Times - A History of the Irish Women's Suffrage Movement 1889-1922,* Dublin, 1984.

Pakenham, Thomas, *The Year of Liberty. The Great Irish Rebellion of 1798,* London, 1969, 1982.

Plath, Sylvia, *Letters Home. Correspondence 1950-1963,* selected and edited by Aurelia Schober Plath, London, Boston, 1976, 1986.

Plath Sylvia, *Winter Trees,* edited by Ted Hughes, London, 1976, 1986.

Powell, T.G.E., *The Celts,* new edition, preface by Stuart Piggott, London, 1991.

Power, Patrick C., *The Book of Irish Curses,* Cork, Dublin, 1974.

Prone, Terry, *Irish Murders. The Shocking True Stories,* Swords, 1992.

Raftery, Joseph, Editor, *The Celts, The Thomas Davis Lecture Series,* Published in collaboration with Radio Telefis Eireann, Cork, Dublin, 1988 edition.

Reuben, David, *Everything You always wanted to know about sex but were afraid to ask,* New York, 1976.

Roberts, Nickie, *The Front Line. Women in the Sex Industry Speak,* London, 1986.

Ross, Anne, *Everyday Life of the Pagan Celts*, London, 1972.

Ryan, John, *Remembering How We Stood*. Bohemian Dublin at the Mid-Century, Dublin, 1975, 1987.

Smyth, Ailbhe, *Women's Rights in Ireland. A Practical Guide*, Swords, 1983.

Somerville-Large, Peter, *Irish Eccentrics. A Selection,* London, 1975.

Spellissy, Seán, *Clare County of Contrast,* Ennis, 1987.

Spellissy, Seán, *Limerick the Rich Land,* Ennis, 1989.

Stengel, Erwin, *Suicide & Attempted Suicide,* Middlesex, 1964.

Stewart, R.J., *Celtic Gods Celtic Goddesses*, London, 1990.

Sullivan, T.D., A.M. and D.B. Sullivan, *Speeches from the Dock or Protests of Irish Patriotism.*

Sykes, J.B., Editor, *The Concise Oxford Dictionary of Current English,* based on the Oxford English Dictionary and its Supplements, Oxford, 1979.

Walford, Edward, *The County Families of the United Kingdom*, London, 1892.

Wallace, Irving, *The Square Pegs,* Great Britain, 1958, Aylesbury, 1968.

White, Carolyn, *A History of Irish Fairies,* Cork, Dublin, 1976, 1992.

NEWSPAPERS, PERIODICALS, ETC.

"AIDS cases increase to over 1m", *The Irish Times*, Wednesday, January 4, 1995.

Allen, Liz, "Too old to live, Too young to die", *Irish Independent,* Wednesday, January 24, 1996.

Anonymous, "Papers on the suicide of Hans Herzogenrath and the attempted suicide of Gertraude Margaret Leopold", unpublished.

Bhamjee, Dr. Moosajee, "The Suicide Bereaved", unpublished.

"Board found negligent in discharging patient without adequate assessment. £35,000 award to family whose father killed himself after leaving hospital.", *The Irish Times,* Thursday, February 1, 1996.

Butler, Maggie, "Therapy, the new religion", *Independent Weekender,* Saturday December 3, 1994.

Cahill, Ann, "Suicide rates soaring among young men worldwide: survey", *The Sunday Press,* January 15, 1995.

Carolan, Mary, "O'Donnell tries to commit suicide during his trial". *The Cork Examiner* 13th March 1996.

Clark, Sarah, and Gwen Singleton, Researchers, *Deathwish: Surviving Suicide,* a booklet compiled by the Community Education Unit at Yorkshire Television, Leeds, for a television programme of the same title which was transmitted on Saturday, 23 May 1993 to coincide with Samaritan Week. The television programme was presented by Craig Charles, produced and directed by Gwyneth Hughes and Pauline Duffy was the executive producer.

Collins, Geraldine, ""Macho suicides" alert as danger seasons nears"", *Irish Independent,* Wednesday, January 10, 1996.

"Coroner's questions at inquest exceeded his powers", *The Irish Times,* Friday, January 27, 1995.

Cowley, Martin, "Another priest at centre of child sex abuse claim" and "North's DPP gets police file on child sex abuse", *The Irish Times*, Monday, November 28, 1994.

Crawley, Jacqueline N., Mary E. Sutton and David Pickar, "Animal models of self-destructive behaviour and suicide", Psychiatric Clinics of North America, Vol. 8, No. 2, June 1985.

Cusack, Jim, "Drug treatment programme for prisoners demanded" and "Four jail suicides and many self-inflicted injuries", *The Irish Times*, Saturday, May 6, 1995.

Cusack, Jim, "Mandatory reporting of sex abuse urged", *The Irish Times,* December 3, 1994.

Dening, Penelope, "Prozac People", *The Irish Times Weekend,* Saturday, May 20, 1995.

Dillon, Willie, "Farmers lead suicide trend", *Irish Independent*, Wednesday, June 29, 1994.

Dodd, Stephen, "Youths who are easy prey", *Sunday Independent*, May 7, 1995."Elderly most prone to suicide", The Irish Post, December 3, 1994.

Government Publications, A statement of the case in favour of the proposed amendment to Article 41.3.2o, of the constitution, Dublin, 1995.

Harman, Alan, "Babies' burial site finally blessed", *The Irish Times*, Thursday, August 11, 1994.

Harman, Paul, "Babies' cemetery will be blessed after 150 years", The Irish Times, Wednesday, August 10, 1994.

Hegarty, Trish, "Call to keep abortion issue out of political arena", *The Irish Times,* Friday, November 25, 1994.

Hegarty, Trish, "If abuse is suspected listen first to the child" and "Teaching children skills they need to protect themselves", *The Irish Times*, Saturday, December 3, 1994.

Hegarty, Trish, "Married men less likely to commit suicide", *The Irish Times,* Tuesday, July 5, 1994.

Hegarty, Trish, "Two Irish children a year die at hands of abusers", *The Irish Times,* Friday, November 18, 1994.

"Highest rate of suicide is among the elderly", *The Irish Times,* Monday, November 25, 1994.

"High-risk time for suicides", *The Irish Post*, August 20, 1994, Hayes, Middlesex.

Holmquist, Kathryn, "Beware paracetamol", *The Irish Times,* Monday, May 16, 1994.

Holohan, Anne, "Bottled up inside", *The Irish Post,* August 20, 1994, Hayes, Middlesex.

Holohan, Anne, "Working Lives", *The Irish Post,* February 18, 1995.

"1,162 abortions show slight quarterly decrease", *The Irish Times,* Saturday, February 3, 1996.

"Irish rate of suicide tops that in Britain", *The Irish Post*, 10 February, 1996.

Kabel, Marcus, "Kohl leaves major posts unchanged in new cabinet", *The*

Irish Times, Friday, November 18, 1994.

Kearon, Kenneth, "Rite and Reason - New law, new twist to euthanasia debate", *The Irish Times*, Tuesday, February 21, 1995.

Kelleher, M.J., P. Corcoran, H.S. Keeley, J. Dennehy and I. O'Donnell, "Original Papers - Improving Procedures for Recording Suicide Statistics", *The Irish Medical Journal*, January/February 1996, volume 89 number 1, Dublin, 1996.

Kelly, Andrew, "Mercy killing of baby "justified" ", *The Irish Times,* Thursday, April 27, 1995.

Kelly, Cathal, "Viewpoint - Alarming suicide rate among young gays", *The Irish Times,* April 24, 1995.

Kennedy, Geraldine, "President signs Bill as court ends legal challenge. Abortion information ruling a boost for divorce poll", *The Irish Times,* Saturday, May 13, 1995.

"Kevorkian at 21st suicide", *The Irish Times,* Monday, 28 November, 1994.

"Limerick immolation", *The Irish Post*, February 3, 1996.

MacCool, Fionn, "A Celtic Myth", *The Irish Post,* February 26, 1995.

Macey, Chris, "Housewives face higher suicide risk. Most men who take their own lives are farmers", *Evening Press,* Thursday, November 10, 1994.

McKay, Susan, "Government muddle on abortion referral", *The Sunday Tribune,* 13 November, 1994.

McKay, Susan, "Much too much, much too young", *The Tribune Magazine,* Sunday, 14 May, 1995.

Mac Uileagoid, Michael, Research Coordinator, and Joseph Baker, Features Editor,"The Executioner in Ireland" and "The Art of Hanging - a Clinical Report", *True Irish Crime. Ireland's Very Own True Crime Magazine,* Issue No.1, Belfast, 1995.

"Man called Samaritans 22 times before suicide", *The Irish Times*, Friday, January 6, 1995.

McElgunn, Joanne, "The bridge of sorrows", *Sunday World*, December 11th,

1994.

McGarry, Patsy, "Doctor says he took part in 50 euthanasia cases", *The Irish Times*, Friday, March 17, 1995.

McGrath, Kieran, "Why child molesters always present themselves as victims", *The Irish Times*, Monday, November 28, 1994.

McNally, Frank, "Messages in the bottle", *The Irish Times,* Saturday, November 26, 1994.

Matthews, Robert, "Scientists discover that suicide is in the blood", *The Sunday Telegraph,* 4 February, 1996.

Moore, Kevin, "Church decline linked to rising suicides", *Sunday Independent,* December 3, 1995.

Mullins, Dave, "An All-Ireland Guide to vice from high-class call girls to street prostitutes there's 1,800 of them making a living in all parts of the country", *Sunday World,* February 5, 1995.

Mulvihill, Mary, "New findings on teenage depression", *The Irish Times*, Tuesday, February 28, 1995.

"Man goes on a roof-top hunger strike", *The Irish Times*, Friday, November 18, 1994.

Moran, Yvonne, "Special report - Suicide", *Evening Press,* Tuesday, February 16, 1995.

"Nine-year-old boy is youngest suicide victim", Irish Independent, Saturday, April 22, 1995.

O' Connor, Imogen, "Grieving a Suicide", *Journal of the Irish Association for Counselling and Therapy* - Suicide, Vol. 1 No. 32, Dun Laoghaire, Spring, 1995.

O'Faolain, Nuala, "Problem kids need a lot more than just fine talk", *The Irish Times,* Monday, November 28, 1994.

O Gadhra, Nollaig, Preacher of Peace", *The Irish Post,* April 9, 1994.

O'Keeffe, Alan, "Tragedy of Viet youth haunted by racial hatred", *Sunday Independent,* April 30, 1995.

O'Leary, Eileen, "Nun's quiet work among prostitutes given recognition", *The Irish Times,* November 18, 1994.

O'Morain, Padraig, "Case of 'Joe Kay' illustrates paradoxes of crisis help lines", *The Irish Times,* January 7, 1995.

"Oregan suicide law blocked", *The Irish Times,* Friday, December 9, 1994.

O'Toole, Gary, "We must stop this man now", *The Sunday Tribune,* 4 December, 1994.

Pallot, Peter, "Decline of village life blamed for farm suicide", *Daily Telegraph,* Saturday, 21 May, 1994.

Pollak, Andy, Religious Affairs Correspondent, "Bishop says media coverage of priest's sex-abuse case was not over the top", *The Irish Times,* November 26, 1994.

Pollak, Andy, Religious Affairs Correspondent, "Hospice doctor tells of how Dutch patients can arrange their own deaths", *The Irish Times,* Tuesday, January 24, 1995.

Power, Brenda, "After a lifetime of rejection, misery and loneliness, Pat Tierney, poet, author, wanderer, street entertainer and AIDS sufferer, went to a churchyard last week and hanged himself. Beforehand, he told Brenda Power why", *The Sunday Tribune,* 7 January, 1996.

Power, Brenda, "Turned against yourself", *The Sunday Tribune,* 30 April, 1995.

Prosser, David, "Suicides by burning in England and Wales", *The British Journal of Psychiatry,* February 1996, Vol. 168, London.

"Psychologist worried by child suicide rates", *The Irish Times,* Friday, November 25, 1994.

Quinlan, Arthur, "Mayor warns on spread of HIV", *The Irish Times,* Wednesday, February 15, 1995.

Reid, Lorna, "Students highest suicide risk", *Irish Independent,* Tuesday, May 24, 1994.

"Report on safety of sheep dips is sought" and "Sheep dip' affects brains", *The Irish Times,* Friday, May 5, 1995.

Rodgers, Paul, Editor, Red Ribbon. *HIV/AIDS and Sexual Health News,* Issue 5 Limerick, April, 1995.

"Samaritans extend service to combat above-average suicide rate", *The Irish Times,* Wednesday, April 26, 1995.

"Sex abusers often need counselling - psychologist", *The Irish Times,* Saturday, November 26, 1994.

Sheehan, Maeve, "Priest dies in gay club", *The Sunday Tribune*, 13 November, 1994.

Sheehan, Maeve, "Priest flees to England after abuse complaint", *The Sunday Tribune,* 11 December, 1994.Sheehan, Maeve, "Third wave of AIDS will hit heterosexuals", The Sunday Tribune, 19 February, 1995.

Sheridan, Kathy, "Smoking is still seen as biggest single risk factor in cot deaths", *The Irish Times*, Saturday, November 26, 1994.

Smyth, Frank, Research Consultant, "Inside Information - Death from above", Unsolved I, Helen Smith, *Death in Jeddah*, London, 1984.

"Suicide verdict on soldier delivered", The Irish Times, Friday, April 28, 1995. *Sunday World,* November 20th, 1994.

"Taylor signs order on stillbirths", *The Irish Times,* Thursday, April 28, 1994.

"The Divorce Referendum", *The Irish Times*, Monday, November 27, 1995.

"The Supreme Court Judgement on the Abortion Information Bill", *The Irish Times,* Saturday, May 13, 1995.

Tindall Gillian, "Blessed Release", *The Times Magazine*, Saturday, March 4th, 1995.

"Transition Times", *The Irish Times*, Wednesday, February 15, 1995.

"Women at Greater Risk", *The Irish Post*, December 3, 1994.

Yeates, Padraig, "Child abuse is investigated at two more centres", *The Irish Times,* Friday, November 25, 1994.

Publications from On Stream available in bookstores or by mail-order:

Suicide The Irish Experience	*Seán Spellissy*	£6.99

Tackling Men's Health, a guide to men's health & fitness.

	Dr. John O'Riordan	£4.99

French Country Roads, a wine-lover's guide to France

	John D. O'Connell	£6.99

Tom Doorley Uncorked! wine guide for purchasing in Ireland

	Tom Doorley	£5.99

Developing On-Farm Research- the broad picture

	Nora McNamara Stephen Morse	£9.99

Memories of Macroom	*James Kelleher*	£4.99
Cobh Now & Then	*Joe Wilson*	£6.50
The Examiner Cookbook	*Editor Roz Crowley*	£5.99
The Man from the Railway	*James P. McNally*	£4.99

Pit Pony Cavallo di miniera

	Gerardo Vacana/Paolo Tullio	£7.50
You May Talk Now!	*Mary Phil Drennan*	£4.99
Brave Seamen of Youghal	*Mike Hackett*	£5.99

For mail-order/delivery send cheque/postal order for cost of the book plus £1.00 to: Mail Order Dept. On Stream Publications Ltd. Cloghroe, Blarney, Co.Cork, Ireland. Tel/fax 021 385798.